Dear Felix
You are Great
Canadian. Thank
you for your support.

[illegible]
~2013~

Foreword by Cora Tsouflidou

GREAT CANADIAN FRANCHISE STORIES

Celebrating Canada's Top Franchisors Success Stories

Felicia Pizzonia with Dawn Mucci

The first in a remarkable series

THE ULTIMATE PUBLISHING HOUSE (TUPH)
CANADIAN HEADQUARTERS
The Ultimate Publishing House (TUPH)
49540 - 80 Glen Shields Avenue, Toronto, Ontario, Canada L4K 2B0
Telephone: 647-883-1758 • Fax: 1-888-673-6398
www.ultimatepublishinghouse.com and www.greatcanadianfranchise.com
E-mail: info@ultimatepublishinghouse.com
Quantity Sales: COMPANIES, ORGANIZATIONS, INSTITUTIONS,
AND INDUSTRY PUBLICATIONS.

Quantity discounts are available on bulk purchases of this book for reselling, educational purposes, subscription incentives, gifts, sponsorship or fundraising. Unique books or book excerpts can also be fashioned to suit specific needs such as private labeling with your logo on the cover and a message printed on the second page of the book. For more information, please contact our Special Sales Department at The Ultimate Publishing House.

Orders for college textbook or course adoption use.
Please contact The Ultimate Publishing House
Telephone: 647-883-1758

TUPH is a registered trademark of The Ultimate Publishing House.
Cover conceptualized by Bebe Bengs, layout by Darlene Dion. Interior design by Darlene Dion.
Printed in Canada.
Great Canadian Franchise Stories, by Felicia Pizzonia with Dawn Mucci.

ISBN: 978-0-615-72169-9

Dedication

Our wish is for all Canadians and people all over the world to read this book and be inspired by all the great Canadian franchisors featured in this book to live their entrepreneurial dream and become the next Great Canadian Franchise Story. Life is meant to be abundant in all aspects, and it is up to you to decide to live your passion now. There is no better time than the present, and as the saying goes, that's why it's a gift!

Wishing you all the best in success.

With Gratitude,

Felicia Pizzonia

Acknowledgment
from Felicia Pizzonia

Gratitude is a powerful emotion that carries understanding, humility and love. There are many people apart from the contributing authors who are involved in creating a book, from the time it is first conceived to the time it becomes a printed bestseller. As a collective we would like to acknowledge their many contributions.

Firstly, I would like to thank Dawn for working with me to create this incredible book; she made the project enjoyable. We all know success breeds success, and I have been honoured and blessed with incredible partners, namely; Dr. Roger Boger, Karen Lauderbach and Tasso Lakas. I am forever grateful for all of them. I would also like to express my sincerest gratitude to my family; my mother and father for their great encouragement and support, to my brother Nat and my sister Vanessa, and all my incredible friends and teachers. Furthermore, I would like to thank my mentors; Bob Proctor, Tasso Lakas, Dino Bottero and Hugh Nicholson.

Last but not least, I would like to thank all the Great Canadian Franchisors who are featured in the first edition of this title; without you this book wouldn't exist. We thank you for sharing your incredible stories with the Ultimate Publishing House and its readers. Always living in gratitude, we hope that everyone's entrepreneurial franchising dreams come true and you too can be part of the next ***Great Canadian Franchise Stories*** book!

Acknowledgment

from Dawn Mucci

First and foremost I would like to thank Felicia for creating such an incredible title, and for introducing me to her publishing house – "The Ultimate Publishing House" – and for working with me on this project. It has been a valuable educational experience and a very interesting process. My passion for franchising, along with the people I have met and worked with in the industry, inspired my desire to help with the book and become an integral part of ***Great Canadian Franchise Stories***.

I would like to thank my family for their loving support, encouragement and patience as I worked on this book. Thank you for allowing me to take the necessary time, focus and resources needed to get the job done. Greg, Barb, Ryan, Diana and Joe; you are all very special and loved. Additionally, I owe thanks to my staff and management team at Lice Squad Canada.

Thank you to the Innisfil business community for your support, specifically The Greater Innisfil Chamber of Commerce, Nottawasaga Futures, and The Township of Innisfil. It is such a great place to do everything including run a business, live in, work in, and play. Special mentions go out to Ned Levitt, Carl Lehman, Ken Leblanc and Ruthie Burd for their mentorship and support.

Finally, thank you to the franchise community the Canadian Franchise Association, CEOs, franchisors, sponsors and educational contributors to the book. Your insight and stories have inspired me and I am privileged to have known and worked with you. You are all Great Canadians in my book.

Foreword

By Cora Tsouflidou, CEO of Cora Group of companies.

I have fond memories of summers past, when I was just a child, the fields filling up with wonderful, small, white balls announcing the long awaited arrival of the clovers. Mom had a knack of making us wait, my sisters and I, but she knew that we would not dare move until we heard her proclaim (by tapping a wooden spoon on an old pot) the official opening of the hunt for four-leaf clovers. So we took off, my two sisters and I, with our eyes as big as saucers, to try to find "the needle in the haystack" which would earn our Mom's praise and, without a doubt, a surprise small treat.

As a teenager, I played this game with the young ones I was babysitting during the summer holidays and later on with my own children who were excited to reenact their Mom's childhood rituals. I have never lost this ability to look for and spot the "out of the ordinary" in a crowd. And this is how I met Felicia Pizzonia and how I distinguished her as a rare find amongst all; one woman full of life, enthusiastic, determined and as promising as the four-leaf clover. To my great surprise was I to find out that not only is she committed to promoting her clients' businesses through her publishing house but she is also searching for four-leaf clovers; the rare people who leave a mark in the business world by their remarkable success. Felicia Pizzonia and Dawn Mucci found eighteen of them in the amazing world of franchising and have asked them to share in this new book their stories, their challenges, and their unusual ambitions. I am positive that every reader striving to succeed in the franchising industry will see themselves somewhere along the path these successful franchisors have walked. And maybe each reader will reiterate the words of the famous author Richard Mabey, who said about the precious four-leaf clover: "an uncommon variation of the common"[1].

Thanks to Felicia Pizzonia and Dawn Mucci, we can all take an intense look at these uncommon variations of franchisors, learn from them and be inspired to reach our own unbelievable peaks.

1 – Flora Britannica, Sinclair-Stevenson, London 1996, p. 225

Table of Contents

Table of Contents

Introduction

What would you say if you were asked which country has the world's largest franchising industry that is second only to the United States of America? If you guessed Canada, you would be right! In fact, the Canadian franchising statistics indicate that for every 450 Canadians, there is a franchise operation up and running. In Canada, the franchise industry represents over $100 billion in sales annually and continues to grow year after year. That means that, one out of every five consumer dollars is spent at a franchise and that about 76,000 individual franchise operations do business in Canada under 900 different brand names. Incredibly, this also indicates that one out of every fourteen working Canadians is employed by a franchise. In addition, new Canadian franchises are popping up every two hours, of every single day, every year!

Learning of these astronomical statistics is what prompted me to write this book on the ***Great Canadian Franchise Stories*** and the many ways this humongous industry impacts Canada and the daily lives of every Canadian citizen. Aside from employing so many Canadians, these franchises provide great opportunities for budding entrepreneurs with little experience to learn the ropes of running a successful business. The skills that these beginning entrepreneurs acquire in the process offers them independence and a sense of great pride and accomplishment when they are able to achieve their goal, of owning their own business. As an already proven business system that has worked time and time again, it equips a new entrepreneur with a blueprint to carve a way to their success while minimizing their risk. The blueprint includes the packaging, artwork, store design, advertising – whether regional or national – as well as, the specific training about the company guidelines, practices, philosophy and more.

Introduction

Maybe you are one of those people that already has an existing business but hasn't been able to master the skills needed to run or grow your business effectively. Or, maybe you want to have a business, but are concerned about taking on the tremendous risk involved in doing so. Becoming a franchise owner enables you to own your business, with minimal risk, since the franchisors have already done the legwork for you and have already done the necessary market research to determine the best future locations and market success probabilities for their brand. As an almost foolproof model, a franchise will enable you to have your business up and running successfully in a minimal amount of time, while lowering the high risk quotient that new businesses incur. This, of course, does not mean that owning a franchise business is completely stress-free, nor does it guarantee that there will not be some challenges along the way. Though, this too is minimized, since as a franchisor you become part of a team that has incorporated within it a great support system. This support system promises you, the entrepreneur, mentoring from experienced and caring people. Due to their own trials and tribulations they have acquired the necessary expertise to guide and mentor you through challenging situations throughout your franchise history. The ***Great Canadian Franchise Stories*** will enlighten you and offers you the ability to learn from the great men and women who have successfully run franchises all over Canada.

Through the years, I have had the privilege of meeting some of these incredibly knowledgeable and deeply spiritual men and women. Most Canadians know about the Pizza Nova, Tim Hortons, Swiss Chalet and some of the different franchise success stories, but I wanted to inspire you by sharing some of the other phenomenal stories of the unlikely entrepreneurs that in spite of their own trials and tribulations successfully grew their concepts into thriving franchises.

The ***Great Canadian Franchise Stories*** is an informative and motivational book that is a celebration of some of Canada's top franchisors and their journey to success. This amazing book garners their candid secrets, their climb to the top and their ultimate accomplishments.

As you delve into the pages of the ***Great Canadian Franchise Stories***, you may already have some preconceived notions about business and franchising. However, if you can set those beliefs aside for some time and plunge into these exhilarating pages with an open mind, you will find untapped wisdom in their stories. You will be able to discover, through their journeys, how to create success and what pitfalls to avoid. You will learn how to leverage your time, money and how to focus your energy. You will be encouraged to listen to your intuition and shown how to follow in their footsteps by preparing a clear and simple plan that will help you manifest your dreams.

If you have the entrepreneurial spirit and want to control your own destiny, it just makes sense to take your idea and to convert it into a franchise concept. Franchising has already created unbelievable opportunities for so many Canadians from all walks of life. It offers you the ability to clone your successful business system and creates residual income for you and your loved ones for years to come. Franchising facilitates the autonomy that everyone so desperately desires, allowing more time for family and the financial stability to pursue your heart's desires. Therefore, it is my hope, that the ***Great Canadian Franchise Stories*** will inspire and motivate you to take your first step towards accomplishing your dream today! Once you make the decision to follow your dream, pursue it whole-heartedly, believe in yourself and create a well thought out plan of purpose that you can stick to. As Napoleon Hill once said, "What you conceive and believe, you can achieve!" So, if you are willing to invest in yourself by putting your heart and soul into your belief, you can start living your dream right now. Who knows… you could become the next Great Canadian Franchise Story!

Happy reading,

Felicia Pizzonia

CHAPTER 1

CORA
Breakfast and Lunch

cora
Breakfast and Lunch

> ***Discipline and focus are the bridge between goals and accomplishment.***

Food is one of life's four basic necessities, but more than feeding the body, it nurtures the soul and leaves you feeling psychologically satisfied. Breakfast literally means to "break a fast" and is, without a doubt, the single most important meal of the day. As founder of the Cora brand, I take my responsibilities very seriously since my name is the brand, and I serve the first bite of food that will ultimately affect your entire day. Many studies have shown that when you start your morning by eating a good breakfast, it sets the pace for a more successful day. With a better disposition you are better equipped to deal with life; you tend to be more focused and you have more energy. I realized that my passion was not only in creative food preparation and presentation, but that my ultimate joy came from bestowing nourishment on others.

My father had always warned me that employment would be scarce for a person with primary interests in literature, Latin, Greek, art, and philosophy. Although I heard his words, fundamentally I am an artist and a dreamer, so I still had to pursue my interests. In my twenties, I left a bad marriage and found myself as a single mom of three with no alimony or child support. I also found out how right my father was when potential employers kept telling me I was either over- or under-qualified for the jobs they had available. Desperate to find a job and in dire straits, I began working at a local restaurant. The work was very hard and we were at poverty level, but at least I was able to provide the basic necessities for my kids. At the same time, although I was grateful to have even a minimal income, deep inside my gut there was a constant desire to improve my financial and material situation. I worked mostly double shifts for five years until a huge burnout sent me to the living room couch to rethink my future. I finally recovered after seven months, with one sole idea: to have my own little restaurant.

I was lucky enough to inherit my mother's creative genes and, like her, I love to create all sorts of new things. I thought I wanted to be a writer, where I could let my imagination go wild and create new worlds for people to explore. One of the most significant things my mother passed on to me was her love for cooking, and that was primarily because it was so transformational. However, I had three teenagers to support and something had to change. When I saw a little snack bar for sale I made a quick decision to purchase it. Based on the facts that I loved to cook, I needed work, and my house was about to be repossessed by the bank, I decided to put the house up for sale. Unexpectedly, a miracle happened and the house sold before the bank took it over.

I distinctly remember that even after all the expenses involved in the sale, the move, and getting a new place to live, I was still able to put a 20% down payment on the restaurant. The four of us moved into a tiny little dwelling, but that didn't matter since most of our time was spent at Cora's anyway. I named the restaurant Cora after my grandmother, who had her own restaurant in her youth. I gave the restaurant a homey atmosphere by bringing in items from home, and whatever else we needed was bought at secondhand stores, which also contributed to the ambiance of the restaurant. All my kids were willing and able to help make Cora's successful; my three teenagers helped me paint our new little store, and we put up the curtains that I lovingly sewed. I also sewed aprons with a sun motif on them for the girls. The old truck stop was now homey, comfortable and inviting just like all our stores today.

The launch date of the first Cora restaurant was on my birthday, May 27, in 1987. From that point on everything changed. Within two weeks of opening I noticed a pattern – the busiest part of our days was breakfast. At that time in Quebec, breakfast at restaurants consisted of a choice of bacon, ham or sausage, a choice of how you liked your eggs cooked, and pancakes. I decided to focus on creating a selection of different breakfast choices, including the huge crepe my mother used to make for us when I was young. Every day I would stop at the Italian grocer across the street and buy fresh fruit for the crepes. The customers were so happy and very encouraging. They were literally eating it all up! At the time, I didn't have any intention of growing the business any bigger. My only motivation was to get us out of poverty and to make enough money so that I could take care of my kids with dignity. Because I strongly believe that you cannot be good at everything, I decided to focus strictly on breakfast, breakfast specialties, and brunch-oriented lunches. It was the best decision I could have made.

When I started offering a greater selection of breakfast dishes, people would say that I had invented new recipes. The truth is that I was simply cooking ordinary dishes in extraordinary ways, like adding chopped spinach to my crepe mix to make a spinach crepe filled with strong cheddar cheese. Before we knew it, Cora's was the talk of the town, even though we only had four tables and a counter, with a total of 29 seats. As the business grew, we also grew our Cora's family by hiring my kids' friends. I remember walking to work and seeing the line of customers wrapped around the building every morning, just waiting to eat breakfast at Cora's. That was a great time as I was behind the counter, connecting with the customers and cooking as they watched. Behind the counter is where the artist in me came alive; instead of writing novels I was creating great tasting food and mouthwatering presentations. The customers loved Cora's and they loved me for creating it!

When I first started the business, I thought that the definition of success was being able to pay my bills and get out of the red at the bank. Soon after we opened the second store, a salesman handed me some placemats and offered to provide me with two months' worth of free placemats. He explained that I could have the Cora logo printed right in the centre of the placemats with our address and phone number, and he would sell some advertising to put on there as well. He was surprised when I asked if I could print two locations on the map. As I looked down at the rectangular placemat I was holding in my hand, I had a vision. I did not see two addresses printed on the mat, but rather the entire map of Quebec was covered with little houses that represented future Cora locations. The only thing missing was the exact addresses of these locations. When I shared my vision with my kids, naturally, they asked how this would happen. I just told them I didn't know but to have faith that it would. It was so ironic; here we were, barely taking $20 a day for gas and expenses and I had visions of a chain of Cora's restaurants dangling in my head. My new mantra became, "Where's the next store?"

As we slowly began opening more stores, I began redefining success as how many people loved my food. That didn't last long since soon thereafter I began to change it again. That was when I caught the entrepreneurial fever, and I became insatiable. As soon as I finished opening a store, I was ready for another and another. It was like going up a big set of stairs that I couldn't stop climbing. Discipline and focus became my new way of life. The more stores we acquired, the more rigorous and focused my discipline became. After the opening of the seventh store, we opened an office in the basement of one of the restaurants, and the ritual of keeping daily count of the customers continued. Since then, every one of our stores has a blackboard in the BOH (back of house) to record their numbers.

I was a scholar not a businesswoman, so when a girl came in asking if she could purchase a Cora's franchise, I had no idea what she was talking about, though I can assure you that I caught on very quickly. What I concluded was that franchising was an excellent vehicle to grow my brand and to open more stores in more territories. As a famous franchisee consultant said, "When you are in the business of selling a product or a service, what you want the most is to sell that product or service in the most stores as possible to the most customers as possible as often as possible." I certainly realized that this was the promise of franchising. I took a full year to read every book on the subject of becoming a franchise and to write the essential documentation it needed. Most of all, it was important for us not to lose our focus of expanding together as a brand and as a family and to remember that it isn't about the money: it's about doing the right thing for the right reasons. Of course we look for franchisees who are disciplined, focused, love people and adore our product. We want people with integrity who want to contribute to their community by creating jobs and a great environment where people will want to gather. Most of all we want them to be excited about growing their own family and business with us. I am thrilled to say that in 2012 we have more than 130 locations from coast to coast, and on average, we serve more than 35,000 breakfasts a day across the network!

I am honoured and humbled to be at the source of such an adventure. It's the best thing that could have happened to me. Success in the end is not how much money you have in the bank or how many rings you wear on your fingers; it is who you become along your journey. I am ever so grateful that I can say I am more secure, more at peace, and more fulfilled because I am living out my purpose and my dreams. The contributions I have been able to give to my family, the community, and even our country has molded me into the woman I have become. I believe that rigorous focus and discipline will get you anywhere you want to go in life. Pleasing people with good food, delighting them with great service, having a warm and welcoming environment, and satisfying their taste buds while infusing their bodies with wholesome nutrition is what we love to do at Cora's.

Cora Tsouflidou

Founder

In 1987, Cora Tsouflidou, a single mother of three in need of a career, bought a small abandoned snack bar in a Montreal suburb as her new business venture. She focused on creating beautifully crafted breakfasts and was soon on her way to launching the chain of restaurants destined to become the country's premiere breakfast destination. Today, the Cora network boasts more than 130 franchise locations across Canada, totalling much higher than ever dreamed in annual sales. With about another dozen locations expected to open every year over the next few years, Cora is leading the expansion of the Cora restaurants. The members of the Cora team are not about to take off their aprons any time soon.

Proclaimed "Queen of Breakfasts" by industry authorities, Cora's achievements have been recognized on countless occasions. She is the recipient and host of entrepreneurial awards and accolades such as the Governor General's Award, the Ernst & Young Entrepreneur of the Year Award in the Manufacturing and Consumer Products Category, the Pinnacle Award, and the Hall of Fame Award from the Canadian Franchise Association. In 2009, she received the Royal Bank of Canada (RBC) Canadian Women Award in the Bell Trailblazer Award category.

Today, Cora still enjoys the success of her challenging yet fulfilling journey. As a spokeswoman, she recognizes the value of extending her knowledge, lessons and passion to other entrepreneurs. Even though in recent years Cora has passed her chair to her son as President of all operations of the chain, she still insists on giving her blessing to all marketing and R&D projects for the brand. Beyond all that, it is still obvious that any time you look at Cora, you cannot help but feel her unconditional love and devotion to her brand.

Cora Breakfast and Lunch

Franchises Cora Inc.
Attention: Franchise Department
16 Sicard Street, Unit 50
Ste-Thérèse, Quebec, Canada J7E 3W8

Quebec Phone: 450-435-2426
Ontario Phone: 905-673-2672
Toll Free: 1-888-673-2672
Email: info@chezcora.com
Website: www.chezcora.com

CHAPTER 2

M&M Meat Shops

LES ALIMENTS

M&M®

MEAT SHOPS

> ***"Be a yardstick of quality! Some people aren't used to an environment where excellence is expected. — Steve Jobs"***

In acting, the best way to memorize lines is to forget everything else that exists in your mind. By becoming the part, you are actually authenticating the role that you eventually assume, though it's the mental energy that brings the role to life.

It's a well-known fact that before actor Jim Carey became famous he always kept a non-negotiable check with his name on it, in the amount of $10,000,000 in his wallet. On a regular basis he would drive to the top of Mulholland Drive and, with outstretched arms holding the check, he would pretend to be rich and famous and scream positive affirmations at the top of his lungs. His career is now marked in history!

Unknowingly, but probably intuitively, we did the same thing! When we first started M&M Meat Shops, we all wore professional-looking white butcher jackets with our names embroidered on them. After all, we were M&M Meat Shops, the modern day butchers! We held our heads up high, always had a positive and welcoming attitude, and never spoke negatively.

We knew that people like to associate with successful people, so, we created the illusion of success. We had our own customized packaging bearing our logo and name, and everyone thought that we were a much bigger organization than we were. Nobody knew that we were purchasing products in restaurant quantities and repackaging everything into smaller pack sizes in the back of the store. We even went so far as to park the one good car in front, while in the back we parked our old, run-down clunkers. Our motto in the early days was, "Think big, act big!" We believed it would become a self-fulfilling prophecy.

I don't think any of us will ever forget February 10, 1981. We were open for nine hours and closed without a single sale at the end of the day. To make matters worse, the cash float didn't balance. My partner, Mark, had taken money from the cash drawer for lunch, and we ended up closing the day at negative $4.50. Yet our continued optimism definitely paid off. Four days after this (February 14th – Valentine's Day), Henry Koch, a local newspaper business writer, wrote a very nice-sized story about the "builder and the lawyer" who sold frozen foods. All of a sudden, the place was jam-packed with customers... so we said, "Maybe we should advertise!"

In the years leading up to M&M Meat Shops, I tried a lot of different careers. Even though I thoroughly enjoyed the variety of experiences, I knew they weren't my calling, yet I didn't know which way to turn. My first degree was in mechanical engineering. By the time I completed the five-year university co-op plan, there were no jobs available. Today, every time I drive by the plant that turned me away, I feel like sending them a "Thank You" card. I quickly deserted that field and decided to study real estate. Three years later, I received my real estate broker's certification, and then my appraiser designation (AACI). Somehow neither of these felt like the right fit for me either.

After abandoning the real estate field, I went into the home building business with my brother Greg, a land developer, and over the next five years we erected about 100 homes as general contractors. It was during this time that I came up with this idea of M&M Meat Shops. We were becoming more and more frustrated by our inability to buy quick, good quality meals at the supermarket. The answer was staring me right in the face: "What if we could bring restaurant-quality foods to the average consumer? We could provide the products that are currently unavailable in the marketplace."

We started contacting different restaurant suppliers in Toronto to find out what products they carried that were only available for the HRI trade (hotels, restaurants and institutions). Unfortunately, the products were also only available in large pack sizes. The next thing we did was enlist the help of our family.

We figured out that if we could take all these high-quality products and offer them to consumers, we could help them get in and out of their kitchens more quickly. We could save them time, not only in food preparation, but also in terms of clean-up too. With women entering the workforce in large numbers, there was a need for quick, high quality meals.

A huge societal shift was emerging around the time we were opening our doors in 1980. Things were very different than years before, when Grandma stayed at home and prepared dinner all day long while Grandad worked. Now, all of a sudden, you had two-income families where both parents were working all day. They came home late and didn't have time to create a meal from scratch. With the convenience of M&M Meat Shops, people could maintain their mealtime traditions, sitting around the table enjoying good food!

The concept we had for M&M Meat Shops was simple. We wanted to create a place where people could purchase choice cuts of restaurant-quality meat and specialty food items at reasonable prices. We started out with 62 products, mostly frozen items that had previously only been available for restaurants and hotels.

Today our product line consists of over 450 items. As we expanded our product line, we started to include single serve portions, classic one-dish meals, upscale appetizers, internationally inspired foods, and amazing desserts. Our products are made of the finest ingredients, and we are constantly changing things up to accomodate the fluctuating needs of the consumer. We offer good taste, exceptional quality, good value, convenience, and to top it off we have the best customer service you can find. Our slogan became, "Hundreds of meal ideas, one aisle!"

What differentiates us from our competition? 1) We have all our own formulations, recipes, products, and special flash-freeze technology; 2) Exceptionally trained customer staff that are product knowledgeable, friendly, and eager to help out with meal planning, food preparation, party planning, nutrition/allergen information, or whatever product advice you need; 3) Storefront parking for quick and easy access to the store. These are some of the key points of differentiation between M&M Meat Shops and the competition. Our mission statement became, "To create a friendly food shopping experience that makes our customers say, 'I'll be back!'"

We used franchising as our model for building out the company. There were a lot of independent food stores popping up all over Ontario, and it was clear to us that if we were going to win the game we had to dominate this niche market. We were right. It didn't take long before we started noticing that the small independents were disappearing, and our biggest competition today is from supermarkets.

We could probably write volumes about the mistakes we've made. This is not unusual for a new business. The important factors are what you learned from those mistakes and how fast you can turn them around. One of the mistakes we made was not to have a franchise lawyer in the first few years we were in business, which resulted in giving away too much territory. We gave away some large tracts of land and had to buy them back later in order to increase expansion in some areas.

To this day, the wonderful connections we've made with franchises, product consultants, customers, suppliers, other franchisors and head offices, are all very important to me. And we are proud to give back to the communities that have contributed to our successes, including our corporate charity, the Crohn's & Colitis Foundation of Canada.

Mac Voisin

Founder

Mac Voisin graduated from the University of Waterloo in 1973 as a mechanical engineer. Unable to find work, he really didn't know in which direction to turn. The fact that he knew very little about the real estate market intrigued him enough to make it his next career choice. After becoming a real estate broker, earning his appraiser certificate and spending three years in this field, he realized this wasn't the right fit for him either. Mac teamed up with his brother Greg, a land developer, to build homes in the Waterloo area. Four years and 100 homes later, Mac had a brainstorm. He was going into the food business, he said jokingly, because unlike home sales, there would always be return business.

Founded in 1980, M&M Meat Shops became one of Canada's most successful franchise operations. Today there are 456 locations across the country, and M&M Meat Shops is Canada's leading retailer of restaurant quality specialty frozen foods. It is also one of the most community-minded companies in Canada. Voisin knows that high quality products are an important component of their success, but most of all, he attributes their success to the outstanding customer service they provide.

"You're only as healthy and happy as the community you live in," says Voisin. "Building a healthy community is not only a privilege, it's my civic responsibility." Voisin has received the Canadian Food Industry's Man of the Year award, the Entrepreneur of the Year by Ernst & Young, Nesbitt Burns and Bank of Montreal, and has been recognized with several Canadian Franchise Association awards, including the Award of Excellence in Franchise Relations and the Corporate Citizen Award for M&M Meat Shops' charity work with the Crohn's & Colitis Foundation of Canada.

For more information on M&M Meat Shops, please visit: www.mmmeatshops.com or contact Patty Attwell (519-895-2580 ext. 448).

M&M Meat Shops Ltd.

Franchise Contact Information
640 Trillium Drive, P.O. Box 2488
Kitchener, Ontario N2H 6M3

Phone: 519-895-2580 Ext. 304
Fax: 519-895-1507
Email: bevr@mmms.ca
Website: www.mmmeatshops.com

CHAPTER 3

Smoke's Poutinerie

"Build it and they will come!"

As an entrepreneur from a very young age, my business philosophy has always been very simple: surround yourself with good people and common sense, and work hard. Since building Smoke's Poutinerie however, I've added two more important components to the list: cleanliness and friendliness. I would also like to clarify that Smoke was my motivation for this business. He is a gastronomical genius, who was really good at conjuring up new mouth-watering concoctions. He is the founder, the man, the myth, and the legend! I was just the lucky stranger that happened to be at the right place at the right time and was destined to live out his dream!

The first venture I started was a property development business with only one rental unit. Within a few years I was able to grow it into a 2,000 unit bundle which sold for a whopping $4 million in assets. Although I dabbled in a few other minor business ventures along the way, my second business was a branding and design firm which I started from scratch. Fortunately, I was able to accrue a list of some prestigious businesses that needed my help with design, i.e., YTV, Nike, Molson, Maple Leaf Sports, etc. Life was good, but even though design and branding was a hot discipline at the time, it simply felt like the right time for me to get out.

Shortly after I sold Amoeba Corp., I realized that I needed more purpose and excitement in my life. I wanted to find myself but I didn't really know where to begin. One day I decided that some death defying feats would get me out of the funk I was in. Bungee jumping was my first attempt at resuscitation. Then I did a lot of wall scaling, rock climbing, and finally skydiving. Unfortunately, or maybe I should say fortunately for me, the very first time, my parachute didn't open! Although my memories are vague, what I remember very vividly was the morning of the fourth day when I saw a man's shadow approaching me from the east and saw his snow boots as they got closer. After determining I was alive, the man picked me up like a sack of potatoes and carried me to his secluded cabin where he nursed me back to life. It was Smoke!

As time passed, we found that we had a lot in common but especially our love of the '80s era and his poutine style cooking. Smoke had a vision of someday opening a poutinerie, which was non-existent until 2008 when I built the first one. Yet, as a recluse it was highly improbable that he'd ever live out his dream on his own. The more we talked about it, the more he encouraged me to build it. All he wanted in return for his idea was for his name and face to be used on the logo of what was to become Smoke's Poutinerie.

Poutine is a traditional Canadian comfort food that would measure right up there with mac'n'cheese or chicken soup. The traditional recipe of fries, curds and gravy has never been modified. Through the years, poutine has mostly been adopted and consumed by Quebecois. As Smoke spoke about his poutine ideas, some of my fondest memories that were associated with eating poutine came rushing back into my mind – like eating poutine at summer camp almost daily, or how after moving to Toronto, road trips were enhanced by the anticipation of stopping at a chip wagon along the way for poutine. I even remembered how, being financially strapped in college, I would make my own poutine, using box dinners such as Hamburger Helper for the foundation. In fact, as far back as I can remember, I have always added ingredients to my one-bowl concoctions.

Smoke and I agreed that although we would never claim to be the inventors of poutine, we would certainly add our own twist to it, and with Smoke's face we were going to introduce it to the world! Having never worked in the food business before, I realized the need to hire a consulting firm that was knowledgeable in systems operations in the fast food business. They saved me a lot of frustration and time by teaching me all about the ins and outs of the kitchen requirements, both for efficiency's sake and for the law, licensing and so on. They were also the "go to" people until I was able to tweak things to my liking.

I learned quickly, since I had no time to spare! We were about to open for business with our poutine being made up of the traditional recipe and a variety of fresh toppings to create custom poutine meals. Our customers could have their pick of our signature sauce, or any other of our twenty different sauces, as well as beef, chicken, pork, and their pick of fresh vegetable toppings. Our absolute guarantee is that everything we serve is fresh, including the fries. For the health conscious, we guarantee that all four food groups are available at all times and that the calorie count per plate never rises above 30,000 calories or goes over 100% fat.

I would have to say that the most monumental day of my life was in 2008, the first day we opened our little 800-foot shop, including the kitchen and seating area. Smoke's Poutinerie was the first of its kind in the world, offering a broad menu based exclusively on poutine. From day one I knew this was the perfect franchise model. It was really a no brainer! I had created an entirely new fast food category and decided to incorporate the '80s theme and music in our branding to make it a fun nostalgic place that people would want to come to. My main focus now was to engage anyone that would listen: the local community, the online community, and the media. I was determined to create a huge buzz around our brand, earning plenty of media coverage by being innovative and newsworthy. I was determined to make poutine the hottest commodity, first in Canada and then in the world.

Before we even opened the doors, Smoke's Poutinerie was being trashed in the media and on blogs. They were writing things like, "Who would ever pay $10 for a poutine?" and "It won't last two months!" However, on that first day, there were lines around the corner even before we opened. Maybe we should have thanked all the naysayers for the publicity. Customers started coming in faster than even I anticipated.

I couldn't fill the orders fast enough, and people were still coming in, in droves. At 2 p.m. on the first day, I decided to shut the doors, but not for the reasons the media gave. On the contrary, the volumes of food we sold in our first few hours of business definitely proved them all wrong. I closed down because we simply couldn't handle the volume. In fact, as soon as we closed the doors I was on the phone ordering a second station and had it installed before we opened the next day. You can only imagine the surprise and elation I felt to find that the demand we encountered exceeded even the high level of revenues that I had anticipated in our initial business plan. In actuality, that is what allowed us to explode in the market so quickly.

The next year, 2009, turned out to be a big year for Smoke's Poutinerie. We opened our second franchise and Smoke sightings were occurring regularly, all over and in the oddest places, like on ballet billboards, as a plumber, and in other unexpected locations. Millions of stickers with Smoke's face were circulating everywhere. Media coverage, TV appearances, and social media were just some of the unconventional ways that we penetrated people's lives. Seeing his face plastered everywhere triggered people's craving for either Smoke's poutine or a hunger to satisfy their curiosity about the hype behind the face. Either way, they ended up at our door, often surprised by our unpretentious, nostalgic, friendly, clean, establishment that served great food. We also launched our 28-foot event catering truck. The bumper-to-bumper plaid-wrapped truck looked so gaudy, it was great! You can see it from a mile away. We also implemented an operations team that was basically geared to introduce classic Quebec poutine to the rest of the world. However, best of all, I created the yearly World Poutine Eating Championships, with our last winner being a professional eater who downed thirteen pounds of poutine in ten minutes.

In three years we have become fifteen franchises strong. We are growing quickly, and the interest in our franchise is gaining speed rapidly. The kind of franchisee that I am looking for is logical, hard working and loves our poutine. The perfect candidate would have work principles that align with ours, is a fun-loving people person who is ambitious and real. I believe the rest will take care of itself as we move towards creating the person's own successful Smoke's Poutinerie franchise business.

Franchising is the gift that keeps on giving! For the franchisee, it is the roadmap to a new life and a better tomorrow. For the franchisor, it is the ability to watch it unfold and know that you are impacting so many people's lives for the better. That is the most rewarding aspect of what we do. It's the same way I feel when mentoring children or giving back to the community. You get more from giving than you get from receiving, but if you can combine the two together, you have it all.

The end to this story is really just the beginning of the chapter for Smoke's Poutinerie and for a fabulous future for many generations of franchises to come. I can attest to the fact that if you truly believe in something, and you build it, they will come! So, how do you like your poutine?

Ryan Smolkin

Founder

Ryan Smolkin's business philosophy is basically very simple: surround yourself with good people and common sense, and work hard. He always believed that "If you build it, they will come!" and they did!

As a young entrepreneur, Ryan started a few businesses from scratch. In his property development business, he started with one rental unit, growing it to 2,000 rental units, and then he sold them as a bundle for $4 million. Just prior to meeting Smoke, he sold his business Amoeba Corp., a branding and design firm. All this was only in preparation for what was to come.

"Friendliness and cleanliness" is Smoke's motto, through the poutine they sell, sprinkled with a bit of tender loving care (TLC), is all it takes to hook you. Stepping into Smoke's Poutinerie is just like stepping into the 1980s. That is the genius of Ryan Smolkin bringing Smoke's gastronomical vision to life. Smoke's Poutinerie is the first of its kind in the world. It offers a broad menu based exclusively on poutine, with '80s music in the background, letter push board menus, and is an experience all its own. The goal of Smoke's Poutinerie is to bring an authentic Quebec classic to the rest of the world. Only a year after opening their shop, the first franchise opened, and in just two years they were on their way to world domination.

Ryan's other love and passion is mentoring college entrepreneur hopefuls and supporting the community on many different levels.

Smoke's Poutinerie

Global Headquarters
85 Kingston Road East, Unit #5
Ajax, ON, Canada L1S 7J4

Phone: 905-427-4444 Ext. 200
Fax: 905-427-9944
Email: franchises@smokespoutinerie.com
Website: www.smokespoutinerie.com

CHAPTER 4

Crabby Joe's Tap & Grill

"Good Food, Good Fun, Bad Temper!"

Since the beginning of time, watering holes have been around in one form or another. Call them restaurants, cafés, tea rooms, pubs, taverns or bars, they have always been a hub for social gatherings and a place of refuge from the pressures of a hard day gone by.

Crabby Joe's was created with that in mind. It is the perfect destination for the hungry and the crabby. We offer good quality food, a comfortable atmosphere and some lighthearted teasing and jokes that are always at Joe's expense. The menu features a mix of family and pub fare, which includes burgers, wraps, steak, wings, and pasta, all served in a casual relaxed atmosphere accompanied by lots of camaraderie. Catering to all of the senses, our ambiance includes mouthwatering aromas, great upbeat music, classic art reproductions, and big screen TVs. We have a mix of booths and tables, and the cozy environment is enhanced by natural brick surroundings, hardwoods, earth tone colour schemes, and accessories that contribute to the character of the dining experience. People of all ages, whether they are sports fans or not, can enjoy Crabby Joe's since there is something there for everyone.

I don't know if it is because of my upbringing or despite of it that I approach life differently. Even in franchising, most people start a franchise for the concept. I was looking for a concept that I believed in so that I could franchise. My intention for franchising was to have a way to help a lot of people in a big way. You see, life was not easy for our family when I was growing up in the villages and mountains of Greece. My parents, who had great attributes, and gave much love and integrity, were extremely poor farmers who could barely keep food on the table for the five of us. The only running water was the little creek behind the two storey rock barn where we lived. We resided upstairs while all the animals, from sheep to chickens, lived below us. We could actually see them, hear them and worst of all smell them through the cracks in the wooden planks of the floor.

When I was twelve years old, we moved to a nearby town with a population of 35,000. It seemed like a whole new world opened up to us. When we moved into our little house with running water and heat, our whole family felt as though we had hit the jackpot. City people teased people from the village about our lack of education and where we lived, but through it all, our parents made us feel loved and continued to walk and talk their life philosophy: take care of your family, work hard, be honest, and help other people whenever you can. The silver lining, although I didn't know it at the time, was that my life's purpose was being realized. I became driven to avert other people's suffering and I wanted to help them find success and joy in their lives.

Soon after we moved into our new location, some of our relatives who had made their way to Canada started to bring the rest of the family to the "land of opportunity".

My parents arranged for my sister to marry at age 17 to a very nice man; my brother was invited to Canada, and when I was 16, I joined him. But that was to be short-lived, since three months later I returned to Greece. I was a kid. I missed my family. I didn't know the language and I really didn't feel that I could acclimate to the new country.

My father, however, had other notions. He basically told me there was no place for me in Greece and that any hope I might have for a brighter future was on the other side of the ocean. He forced me to go back. So at 17, with no other option, I returned to Canada with some newfound hope and the intention of making my family proud.

As it turned out, my first employment opportunity was also my biggest source of education. Although I had only nine years of total schooling, here I got to learn the hospitality business from the kitchen bottom up. In time, I worked my way up and found that I had become operationally driven. I also developed my attention to detail and saved every cent that I could spare. My brother and I decided to combine our resources and eventually bought a sub shop together. At 21, I was introduced to my beautiful Greek soon-to-be wife who happened to have come from a similar background as my own. I had my business, and she had just graduated from university and life was looking up. Inside, though, I still had a burning fire to help others like me overcome their painful roots and to watch them succeed!

In the early 80s, my brother and I decided to sell the sub shop and began opening and operating a chain of corporate family restaurants. When we accumulated twelve restaurants we decided to sell them, split the profits, and independently pursue our dreams. It was finally my time to be able to help others, and franchising looked like the solution. I knew my calling had always been based on a deep determination and motivation to help people succeed. I also knew that I specifically wanted to help people who didn't have previous business experience in the hospitality industry. Another idea I had was to create a team of like-minded individuals, including our franchisees and business partners, who could contribute their input and ideas.

Looking at my life, dreams, ideas, goals, and the motto which I live by, I realized how blessed I was with the great wife, team, and support staff that helped turn my aspirations into reality. I wanted to put together and share the success of a system and the concepts that I believed in. Franchising was the perfect career for me since it is all about building relationships, meeting new people, seeing people succeed, and helping people meet and share their dreams. But I still needed a concept that would be "franchisable." So with the help of some colleagues, friends, and a marketing firm we developed my basic but premature concept and created a themed restaurant that was fun and comfortable, serves great quality family-style food, and named it "Crabby Joe's Tap & Grill."

There's a saying that "creativity is not the finding of a thing, but the making something out of it after it is found." In 1996 we opened our first Crabby Joe's Tap & Grill. I believe that the most important thing franchisors need to do for their franchisees, is to provide them with the best operational support and tools they will require to achieve success. We need to ensure and protect their investment by maintaining the brand's standards and consistency across each franchised location and throughout the entire system. We need to educate them, and we need to be there for them when they need support, training, coaching, etc. We also need to understand what they are going through, all while consistently improving the company and the concept.

Obsidian Group Inc. is a management company I formed that encompasses professionals who are available to support the franchisees on every level. It was formed for development purposes, and for marketing and managing the hospitality and real estate interests. The team is made up of impressive key hospitality professionals and experienced management personnel in operations, human resources, real estate, construction, marketing, accounting, franchising, culinary arts, etc. They are all in-house, hands-on, hard-working, dedicated individuals who have an entrepreneurial background and who share a common vision of success.

We began managing Crabby Joe's Tap & Grill right from the start, as well as our two other franchises: Coffee Culture Café & Eatery in 2006 and Union Burger in 2010. And, as our family continues to grow, so does our brand awareness, business values, public relations, purchasing power, and most importantly, our customer count. Today, Obsidian Group Inc. is one of Canada's fastest growing and most progressive hospitality companies, and it is described by the media as being "unlimited"!

Between restaurants, gas stations, grocery stores, and even the car you drive, at some point during your day you are interacting with at least one franchise system. However, franchising is not for all character types. Franchising is designed for people who are entrepreneurial, but understand and can operate within a pre-designed system. I would advise future franchisors to be very careful at the start, to have a vision, to stick with it, and to ensure they make as few mistakes as possible. They should seek advice but not be influenced by other people, since it is very important for individuals to stay true to themselves. This is especially true when analyzing their individual character type and whether or not they have a personality that will enable them to flourish within a franchise system.

At Crabby Joe's we are always looking for hard-working individuals with good character and integrity. We want people who care for their business and are willing to do what it takes to be successful. We look for individuals who have demonstrated success in either owning or managing a business with a large number of people. They must be able to manage finances and be committed and disciplined enough to be involved hands-on and full-time in managing the day-to-day operations of the franchise. They need to understand every aspect of their business and to be in touch and know what is happening in every department. In addition, the franchisee must also be able and willing to train and motivate the restaurant employees to deliver an exceptional and consistent guest experience.

My vision for Crabby Joe's is to expand across the country and into the United States through a methodical process whereby we can maintain the operational standards of the brand without over extending our staff, suppliers, manufacturers, distributors, business colleagues, and franchisees. For my kids, I wish a happy balanced life where they can find their passion and fill their days with hard work that fulfils them. For me, I knew my calling has always been based on a deep determination and motivation to help people succeed. I am grateful for the poverty I came from and for the great assets that my parents gave me. I deeply appreciate my father's wisdom, love, and the emotional courage it took to send me back to Canada. All of this kept me humble. For now, I am driven by the continuation of our franchisees' successful relationships and growing businesses, and a profound fondness of seeing newcomers as they rise to their potential.

Gus Karamountzos

Founder

Gus Karamountzos was born in Karya, Greece on October 2, 1960. He was the youngest of three children, the oldest a sister and the middle child a brother. He was raised in a small village in extreme poverty. Gus' father was a farmer, and his mother helped out where she could along with all of her household chores. When Gus was 10, the family moved to a bigger town with a population of 35,000. There the family was able to start a new way of life and were fortunate to take advantage of the education that was available to them at the time.

In 1977 at 17 years old, Gus was encouraged by his parents, but especially his father, to join his brother in Canada in an attempt to make an even better life for himself. His father knew that there would be more opportunities in Canada and he wanted the brothers to reunite. Although he left behind a lot of family members, including his father, mother and sister, Gus ventured into the world to create a new and better life for himself.

Gus immigrated to Stratford, Ontario where he joined his older brother, along with a

few distant relatives who had left Greece before he did. He worked in restaurants in odd jobs in the kitchen and as a cook. He met Helen, a beautiful Greek woman, whom he married in 1982 in Toronto, where she lived and had just graduated from Ryerson University. In 1983, they celebrated the birth of their first son, Peter. In 1984, a second son George was born and in 1988 his daughter, Tina, joined the family too.

While raising his family, Gus put all his efforts into working and building equity so that he would be able to survive and raise a family. Helen mostly stayed home raising the children along with help from the children's grandparents, and she helped Gus as much as possible in the family-operated restaurant. Gus continued to open individually operated restaurants. With his experience, his passion for food and cooking, and his experience operating the kitchens, he was able to operate each of the restaurants and made enough to provide for his family. It was his passion for the restaurant business, his commitment, drive and perfectionism that led Gus into many business opportunities, including Crabby Joe's Tap & Grill, Coffee Culture Café & Eatery, and Union Burger.

As the years went by, after many sacrifices and relocations, Gus and his family made the Greater Toronto Area their home and business headquarters, which today manages and operates more than 250 properties and restaurant locations throughout Canada and the United States.

Crabby Joe's Tap & Grill

2556 Meadowpine Blvd.
Mississauga, ON L5N 6P9

Phone: 905-813-8030
Email: info@crabbyjoes.com
Website: http://www.crabbyjoes.com/

CHAPTER 5

Master Mechanic
Professional Auto Services

> **"*It takes 8,460 bolts to assemble an automobile, and one nut to scatter it all over the road. — Unknown*"**

For many of us, the automobile is the largest investment a family has outside of their home. When it comes to servicing and maintaining this sizable asset, there are definitely many choices out there. We can search a lifetime for the right professional… one that we trust… one that provides practical advice… one that is technically competent… one that we truly enjoy doing business with. Once we find that person, we want to stick with them. Is it any different from having that relationship with your doctor, dentist, hairdresser, financial advisor or lawyer?

And let's face it… many people love their cars! After all, an automobile fulfills our ego, provides us with safe and dependable transportation and the freedom to roam. So finding the right service provider is important to us.

When automobiles were first invented, the same people who had been repairing horse drawn wagons and carriages also fixed the newly produced automobiles. As time went by, though, the automobile engine became more complex and sophisticated. This has escalated the automotive repair industry into one of the most technically demanding careers. Today's technicians require considerable training in order to keep pace with the manufacturers' continued bombardment of new technology. They must inspect, diagnose, and correct sophisticated electronic systems on a multitude of domestic and foreign cars. Initially, it was thought that computers would reduce the need for skilled labour, but in reality the opposite has been proven to be true. The bottom line is, fixing today's automobile requires greater skill and is simply not for the "do it yourselfer" (DIYer). That's why Master Mechanic was created. Jamie and I acquired the Master Mechanic franchise system in 2004 from the originator, who wanted to retire.

After a 16-year stint as a chief financial officer (CFO) in the vehicle leasing and fleet management business, and after a number of acquisitions as the "acquiree," the most recent of which was GE Capital, I realized that the large corporate world and lifestyle was not for me. I wanted to return to small business with a far wider scope of involvement and at the same time improve my quality of life.

Coincidentally, during the process of my search for the perfect small business in which to invest, I ran into Jamie when we volunteered to chaperone our kids' kindergarten pumpkin picking event. We had known each other about eight years at this point in our lives because we shared a passion for vintage cars. Jamie had been involved in Master Mechanic for the prior 20 years, both as a franchisee and right at that time as the General Manager of the franchisor.

It had always been Jamie's desire to eventually buy the business from the original owner, but admittedly he needed assistance to manage the business. As our conversation continued, we discovered that between the two of us, we had all the skills necessary to make a great team. Jamie had the technical, operational, and hands-on background, while I had the finance, administration, marketing, and general business management background. It was the perfect fit, with virtually no skill overlaps. We could make this happen and so we set out on our mission!

Heading into this venture in our mid 40s certainly had an element of risk, as we put everything on the line, including our families, who were dependent on us. We spent countless days on due diligence and financial sensitivity analysis, which allowed us to mitigate and control worst case scenarios... but this is what you must do to understand both your upside and downside with any business venture. At the end of the day, the economics made sense, and the cash flows supported the leveraged debt financing. We believed the business had a sufficiently solid foundation on which to build with its 36 locations and strong reputation in the marketplace.

There were learning curves along the way, as in every business, whether it is a franchise or not. One of the things that comes to mind is the traditional mindset and way of thinking in this industry. For example, our industry would typically target B or even C type sites, which are considered back street locations where strong retail visibility is nonexistent. Such a location could afford an owner more square footage for less rent, but the savings are only offset by an increased marketing budget in an effort to drive customers to your store. Today, we are only interested in A type sites with good retail exposure. Another example of traditional thinking in our industry was to only recruit franchises who were mechanics, whereas today we are in fact targeting those with business backgrounds, so you don't have to be a mechanic to be a Master Mechanic.

One of the monumental things that we did was to alter the traditional and outdated marketing strategy. We increased our national advertising investment and we are continuously encouraging our franchises to follow suit in their own respective markets.

In 2006 we created our memorable jingle. One day, I was wearing my Master Mechanics' jacket at my son's sporting event. As I was holding the door open for this group of 12-year-olds, some of the kids noticed my logo and started to sing our jingle. My heart smiled when I realized that what we set out to accomplish with the jingle had worked, especially if young teens knew all the words and were singing it.

We are proud to say it's ours, and we take everything very personally with regard to our franchises because we truly want each and every one of them to be as successful as they can possibly be. It is a fact that the franchise model in our country delivers a higher probability of success than independent brandless businesses, and our business is no different. Franchising quite simply works well in our industry. We get the biggest thrill from witnessing franchises embrace and adhere to our program and franchise systems, and are successful because of it.

What are some other ingredients for a successful franchisee? One is being able to work "on" your business rather than "in" your business. Working "in" your business means you've simply bought yourself a job; working "on" your business requires continuous focus on management, development, and measurement. We are huge believers in performance measurement because it is imperative to understand the math and the matrixes of your business. As the old adage goes, "You cannot manage what you cannot measure." We train our franchises on performance measurement: how to calculate, compare to benchmarks, how to strive for targets and practical approaches to improvement.

As an owner of a small business, we believe you must be hands-on and active day-to-day in your business as this is the essence of small business. Being a passive investor and hiring someone to run the business for you, just doesn't cut it. If you want the executive role, then go buy yourself a medium-sized business.

We believe, as a franchisor, it is important to treat each franchisee as an individual since they are not all the same. Just as we encourage them to have personal rapport with their customers, it is important for us to have good relationships with them. We want our franchises to know they can depend on us to support them in every aspect of their Master Mechanic business. We have a lot of experience and even more solutions. We have a great training program and we want them to know that we are a business family, just a phone call away from the answers and support they need.

We heard a great quote a number of years ago and it's stuck with us. That is, "do ordinary things in an extraordinary way". It's not about just meeting customer expectations, but rather, exceeding them every time; it's not about settling for mediocrity, but rather, striving for greatness. Great customer service is an attitude and a culture, and it is what will differentiate us from our competitors. Our primary goal is to seek long-term relationships with each of our clients through committed service excellence and business integrity, and by taking a unique personalized approach. Hence our slogan: *"At Master Mechanic, you talk to the mechanic."*

Hugh Welsford
President

and

Jamie Holmes
Vice President

Hugh Welsford has been a chartered accountant (since 1986) and President of Master Mechanic since March 2004. For the 15 years prior, his role was Vice President of Finance for GE Capital Fleet Services (including predecessor companies such as Associates Fleet Services and BML Leasing). He was part of the senior leadership team in this vehicle leasing and fleet management business. He is a Director and Officer of the Corporation.

Jamie Holmes, Vice President, is a Class A licensed mechanic, ASE Master Technician (Automotive Service Excellence). He joined the corporation in May 2000 as General Manager of Operations. He owned and operated the first franchise granted by Master Mechanic. Prior to having joined the corporation, he devoted his full time to the management of his franchise. He is a Director and Officer of the Corporation.

Master Mechanic Head Office

3250 Ridgeway Drive, Unit 1
Mississauga, ON L5L 5Y6

Phone: 905-820-2552
Fax: 905-820-2558

Franchising Opportunities
Hugh Welsford
Phone: 905-820-2552 Ext. 208
Fax: 905-820-2558
Email: Hugh@mastermechanic.ca
Website: www.mastermechanic.ca

CHAPTER 6

Sangster's Health Centres

The natural choice for health

> *PPF! Put Your Partners First!*

While most stores sell products, we sell solutions, prevention, and most importantly, hope! The Sangster's concept was not initially my idea, though I feel extremely fortunate to be born into the Sangster entrepreneurial legacy. In 1960, my grandfather Wallace, introduced my father to the health store concept when he purchased such an establishment in Saskatoon from a man who had cured himself of cancer by ingesting vast amounts of alfalfa in tea and in tablet form.

Thomas Edison once said, "The doctor of the future will give no medicine but will interest his patients in the care of the human frame, in diet and in the cause and prevention of disease." Although my father never claimed to be a doctor, he believed in the same philosophy. So in 1971 it was my father, Roy, who founded Sangster's in hope of helping people "make health a habit!"

At the time, the percentage of the population that purchased health foods was very small, but that was changing rapidly. Seeing the potential of this industry in the mid '70s, my father, who was obviously ahead of his time, made the decision to franchise. He opened his first franchised store in Saskatoon, Saskatchewan. Sangster's advantage began when my dad introduced his own exclusive line of vitamins and supplements, which helped expand and strengthen our company.

One of my first childhood recollections was at school trying to explain my father's job, entrepreneur, to my teachers and classmates. I had never seen anyone in my family work for someone else. It wasn't until years later that I realized how I had been groomed to follow in my family's footsteps. I can still hear the words that my father must have repeated over a thousand times in my early childhood, "You're a leader, Darryl!" and "Always be conscious of your actions because others are watching and following your lead."

Looking back on my life, I can see how these positive reinforcements profoundly molded my character, my direction, and fueled my confidence in so many aspects of my life. It really was no wonder that I took on leadership roles from junior high on up, and as I grew I learned that you don't have to be nice to be respected. All you need is to be strong, honest and fair.

Even though I grew up in the family business and was groomed for this all my life, I still had to work my way up the ladder. So in 1996, when our entire company was made up of only seven head office staff, I started with Sangster's, physically picking, packing and stocking the warehouse, before gaining real on-site experience opening new franchised locations throughout Canada. I didn't mind at all; on the contrary, I learned whatever I could and I invested my time in focusing on vertically integrating the entire organization, from manufacturing to the consumer experience. In 1998 a position in purchasing and inventory control became available, and I took a split position where I controlled both the buying and advertising for Sangster's. In late 1999, the company once again made some moves within the organization to help stabilize and control its growth, so I took on yet another position. I became a full time marketing and advertising manager of three staff members in purchasing and two warehouse staff. By 2002, the company restructured its growth once again, which included moving me into a permanent managerial position, making me accountable for the productivity and actions of two advertising/marketing staff, three sales staff, and a corporate manager. In 2008, I was honoured with my father's trust, respect, and blessings, supported my desire to become the next president of Sangster's Organization.

The franchising business model was already in place when I entered the Sangster's picture in 1996. However, I am a strong advocate of the franchise structure as opposed to a corporate structure. One of the most monumental moments in my life was when I asked a very successful man sitting next to me at a charity event to what did he attribute the success of his empire. Without hesitation he answered, "PPF!" It's been my motto ever since. "Put Your Partners First!" he said to me, "and if you do that, business is easy!" His profound message simply meant that by helping my franchises to become successful and profitable, our organization will benefit too since it becomes like a perpetual "Pay it Forward" system that always boomerangs back to you. Franchising is the perfect model for that. It allows us to mentor people with our concept and help them enjoy the fruits of their labour by becoming successful business owners. Best of all, though, is the joy I get from watching a franchisee escalate the quality of their life by using our proven system, which revolves around natural health products and education.

I can tell you that having a solid support system is imperative. I was taught that mistakes, failure, and change are all OK as long as you face them honestly and learn from them. I can also tell you that it's so much easier when you have someone there to break your fall. I have been very blessed to have supportive people around me, especially my wife and my father. My dad is an incredible business man in addition to being my mentor. I would regularly bounce ideas and strategies off him throughout my life, but especially during those months of negotiating my eventual purchase of Sangster's. I am incredibly blessed to have my wife, who has been my rock, and she too was especially strong during the nine months of excruciating negotiations. I had drawn up four separate "Offers to Purchase" in this time period. This meant that during these negotiations, not only did our deal to purchase Sangster's fall through, but our dreams collapsed on three separate occasions as each offer fell apart. The support of my wife during that time was nothing less than awesome. When I was down, distant, mentally drained, stressed to the hilt, and at times unreachable, my wife kept encouraging me. Not once did she tell me to quit.

On another occasion, only a month after we closed on this amazing purchase of Sangster's, the opportunity to purchase a manufacturing facility presented itself. Even though it would completely clean out our savings and put us at the mercy of financial lenders, she never wavered and encouraged me to keep going.

The big shift for Sangster's began in February 2010 when my wife and I were fortunate enough to successfully purchase Sangster's back from the publicly traded company, Planet Organic Health Corp (POHC), as well as purchase a manufacturing facility here in Saskatoon. We approached the commitment to the manufacturing facility as a critical piece of our Strategic Initiative, which was, and still is, to continuously fulfill our Mission Statement through positive change. Our ultimate vision is to provide natural choices through quality products, to educate, and to advise people about living a healthy lifestyle. The purchase and subsequent development of our manufacturing facility in June was the missing piece to our development goal of a truly "vertically integrated" system consisting of a manufacturing facility, a central distribution warehouse, a licensed franchise system, and retail store fronts. We were now in the business of manufacturing our own health products: vitamins, herbs, natural and organic functional foods, flax seed, hemp seed, etc., right here at home. This, of course, afforded us the ability to expand our company both financially and internally.

Our goals and ideas were never singular events. The strategy we implemented was based on decade-long strategies which involved our core belief system (first and foremost PPF) and leadership initiatives, along with our ten commandments (our CORE values):

- Build open and honest relationships with communication
- Pursue growth and learning through hard work
- Deliver "WOW" through exceptional service

- Be optimistic, creative and open-minded
- Be passionate, accountable and focused
- Build a positive team with family values
- Embrace and drive positive change
- Respect and trust each other
- Create fun and excitement, and lastly,
- Do more with less!

We recognized that leadership trickles from the top down, therefore, I am responsible for what is communicated and taught to our employees. That is supported with tangible components such as our mission, our core values, and our vision. The result of true leadership is that the staff and partners unanimously believe that they are all an intricate part of a bigger culture.

I believe the most significant and noticeable change cycle for our franchise system has just begun and is yet to come! In January of 2012 we embarked on merging our two separate buildings into one, thereby further improving the logistics and communication in the process of building an even stronger foundation as we work our way towards fulfilling three generations of visions for Sangster's. It's ironic and amusing to read in clarity our visions marked in a short excerpt on the history of medicine, proving once again that history repeats itself as it comes back full circle:

2000 BC – "Here, eat this root!"

1000 BC – "The root is heathen, say a prayer!"

1850 AD – "The prayer is superstition, drink this potion!

1940 AD – "The potion is snake oil, take this pill!"

1985 AD – "The pill is ineffective, take some antibiotics!"

2000 AD – "The antibiotic is artificial, eat this root!"

2012 AD – "...people are getting it!"

Today we are so very proud to say the Sangster's Organization is Canada's longest running health and nutrition franchise with over 40 locations in Canada, specializing in sales of dietary supplements (vitamins, minerals, herbs, oils, powders, drinks), organic and non-organic foods, health and beauty products, natural source cosmetics, personal care products, and fitness and nutrition products, in order to provide natural health choices. To ensure a high quality product, Sangster's manufactures over 360 exclusive products in Canada exceeding the industry's standards. Every Sangster's location also carries a wealth of free informational literature on hundreds of natural health issues, including Sangster's exclusive magazine *Natural Living*. I guess, in our own way, we are bringing Canadians back to the "roots" of healthy living.

Darryl Sangster

President and CEO

1992 – Darryl graduated from Athol Murray College of Notre Dame. Played Junior Hockey in Yorkton, SK., Minor Pro Hockey for the San Antonio Iguanas and ended his hockey career playing in Germany.

1996 – Started working at Sangster's.

1999 – Completed a two year course at the University of Saskatchewan.

2002 – Married his beautiful wife Cindy.

2003 – Completed the Canadian Securities Course for investing.

2007 – Earned his private pilot license.

2008 – Completed the first of two triathlons.

2012 – His goal is to compete in his third triathlon.

Darryl Sangster is most known professionally as the president and CEO of Sangster's, which is the retail face of the corporation. Unknown to many is that

Sangster's Corporation is an intricate mix of professional divisions comprised of a franchise licensing division, a warehouse distribution division known as Darwen Holdings, a real estate leasing division known as S-5 Holdings, and a supplement manufacturing division known as Canadian Bio Manufacturing.

In 2005, Darryl became the Vice President of Business Development, which involved overseeing all aspects of operations within the company and reporting directly to the President. By early 2007, Roy and Darryl began building a succession plan for the company, and Darryl spent most of 2007 as Roy's protégée in training. On January 1, 2008, Planet Organic Health Corporation officially accepted Darryl's proposal and plan as the next president of Sangster's Organization, which also led to his father's retirement later that summer.

Two years later, on February 19, 2010, Darryl and Cindy were successful in purchasing Sangster's Organization back from Planet Organic Health Corporation, thereby making Sangster's a privately owned family business once again. As the current president & CEO of Sangster's, Darryl pushed to acquire Canadian Bio Supplements – a local manufacturing company – in order to efficiently manufacture and control Sangster's product quality and supply. On July 1, 2010, Sangster's was successful in acquiring Canadian Bio Supplements which currently manufactures about half of all Sangster's Brand Supplements.

Sangster's Health Centres Franchise Head Office

2218 Hanselman Avenue
Saskatoon, Saskatchewan
Canada S7L 6A4

Phone: 1-877-653-4481
Email: franchise@sangsters.com
Website: www.SangstersFranchise.com

CHAPTER 7

Lice Squad Canada Inc.

Lice Squad
CANADA™
Parent & Teacher trusted!

"Changing the way people treat head lice one head at a time."

Some people take a lifetime to figure out their purpose and to find their passion. I knew from a very young age that I was born to be an entrepreneur. As soon as I could count I started running successful lemonade and product stands from the foot of my flat above the record store in the High Park area of Toronto, where I grew up. I sold anything I could find or make. I was a creative spirit, and I did quite well as an independent kidprenuer. That entrepreneurial bug never left me. I knew fundamentally in my heart that I needed to create and add value. I believed in my imagination and I discovered early on in life how to be persuasive. I recall convincing my childhood best friend that I was Pippi Longstocking and that we could both fly. He proceeded to jump off a garage roof and broke both his arms and a leg. From that point I used my powers of persuasion only for good.

My story begins when I experienced head lice as a little girl. I spent many days in my room crying because I was brutally teased and humiliated. I never understood why I always got lice. Now I know that it was because I was such a sociable child. I had long, thick, clean hair, which made me a prime target. When lice struck me again as a mother, I went looking for help. It was during that time that I had an epiphany. No child or person should ever feel bad about having head lice, and there had to be a better way to deal with it. What troubled me was that I found no help and the recommended treatment was to use a pesticide. That made no sense as I was well aware of the potential dangers associated with the use of pesticides. Why were they still being recommended for head lice and put on children? Also, I could help my child, but who was going to help me get them out of my hair?

I began to seek alternatives to my situation and unknowingly was in the infancy of doing market research for what would ultimately become a new business. I felt a positive energy about what I was doing. My being felt electric, like the feeling you get when you fall in love. You just know when something is right. I was on a mission with the purpose of turning my bad situation into something of value to myself and others.

I started Lice Squad Canada in 2001 as a single mother with $500 dollars to my name. As I was not privileged to go on to higher education, it was a challenge and another stigma that I had to overcome. Lack of education never caused anyone starvation or failure, but a lack of motivation and persistence has. So I took the risk despite any doubts and fears that I had. I believed in myself and what I wanted to accomplish. My level of pedigree comes frankly from hard work, persistence, and a calling in my soul to create and contribute. I consider myself a renaissance entrepreneur with a myriad of talents and skills that I gleaned from a variety of people, experiences, and circumstances. I relied on my creativity, ingenuity and imagination, and turned to my local business development centre for help.

I was cognizant of my abilities and focused on my strengths, delegating tasks where I had little skill or understanding. Since franchising is the fastest way to grow and organize a business, I chose to grow my business using that model. With my passion, enthusiasm and persuasion, I began to attract people who wanted to operate a lice business under my brand. In 2002, about a year after refining my system, I sold my first franchise to a woman in Sudbury. She is still with me today.

I am probably not the first to admit that being a franchisor is a tough gig. It certainly is not for the weak of spirit and requires a lot of fortitude. If you do it right, the rewards are amazing. I was a rookie forging into a new territory so I had to start from scratch (so to speak) and figure it all out. I recall the days when I had to wear most of the hats in the day-to-day operating of the business. I became exhausted really fast and made many mistakes. Looking back it would have been ideal to have a partner or to delegate more, but in those early days you do what needs to be done within the budget you have. Those challenges and experiences refined my character, gave me courage, and taught me discipline. They also afforded me a real world practical education, like learning the art of negotiation, which I used to better my franchise offering and myself as a business woman.

The Lice Squad Canada brand is unique. My vision is to change the way people treat head lice and to be a valuable and vital community resource. The company's mission is to break the stigma associated with head lice and to stop the overuse and abuse of pesticides on children and our planet. This defines the brand, as does our culture of people helping people with positivity, passion, purpose, and pleasure, ultimately leaving the customer with peace of mind. It is a lifestyle that resonates with the community. A motto I've always tried to live by and the foundation for my life and business is to treat others as you wish to be treated. When it comes to stigmatized issues, people find comfort in acceptance and understanding. I want people to walk away from an experience with Lice Squad Canada with that very feeling and with a sense of empowerment.

Over the years Lice Squad Canada has been recognized with many awards. The ones that mean the most to me are for customer service. I contribute to national children's magazines, websites, television shows and newspapers on the topic of head lice. Education is essential, and people have a lot of questions. My franchises have been fortunate to get a great deal of exposure because of this, and it is my pleasure to work hard for that exposure because I know they appreciate and benefit from it. A few examples are features in *MacLean's* magazine, The Discovery Channel, Breakfast Television, CBC, CTV, Global, *The National Post*, *Toronto Star* and *Sun* newspapers, *Franchise Canadian Magazine* and *Today's Parent*. Lice Squad's website is one of the top ranked and referred to websites for head lice. I am very thankful for the relationships that I have been able to form with my media and community partners. I have a great deal of respect and appreciation for them. Knowing that my job is to help them is a big part of that relationship. Time is precious and people have a lot coming at them. You have to make it easy.

Subtle is sweet in the head lice business. Trust, a good reputation, and quality care are the keys to opening doors that form lasting and fruitful relationships. Lice Squad's confidentiality guarantee resonates with clients. It is also why I take my time to find outstanding providers. Clients have the assurance that as a franchise system our standards are consistent and the services we provide are uniform. There is peace of mind in knowing that all of our providers adhere to protocols created to protect them and offer the very highest in quality care. We treat clients like family and that translates into word of mouth referrals for which we are all most grateful.

A monumental lesson that I learned about franchising was to surround myself with the right partners and to understand the laws associated with franchising. I admit that I learned that lesson the hard way. A franchisor needs to make it clear in the disclosure document and franchise contract what the responsibilities and obligations are on both sides and remain firm and consistent with them. Don't promise more than you can deliver, and don't compromise the integrity of what was agreed. This is done for the benefit of both the franchisor and franchisee. Be careful who you agree to do business with. All parties need to be involved in a franchise for the greater good of the company as a whole. If not, self-interest and personal agendas will stifle the growth and betterment of the whole system. It pays to quickly identify and steer clear of users, victims, unbelievers, know-it-alls and those who have trouble following a system. It is also important to know how to mediate and openly work out any issues that may arise. Franchising is about working together toward a common goal, sharing resources and then sharing the gains.

Thanks to franchising, Lice Squad Canada has helped over one million Canadians overcome head lice and has spared many children from unnecessary pesticide exposure. My persistence to continue down the franchise road despite the challenges that I have faced has allowed me to provide meaningful careers and a good living to people and a valuable community service. Lice Squad Canada will celebrate 12 years in business in 2013. I could not have done that without the many people that I met in the industry who acted as partners, mentors and supporters.

I encourage anyone interested in franchising to do their homework. Pick a franchise system that suits your personality and a franchisor you can relate to. No one gets to where they are in life or business on their own. People manage better and succeed faster with structure, support and mentorship. I love the sense of community and being part of something bigger than myself. My ideal franchise partner is hard-working, honest, with business and management acumen. Passion and a good work ethic to deliver the brand's product, mission, vision, and culture are essential. I want healthy, energetic, and driven people with family support who are active members of their community and are not afraid to pick up the phone and connect. As with any business, change is constant but one thing that does not change is my desire to find people with PEPP. It's an acronym that describes the ideal person for the Lice Squad franchise team. It stands for Passionate, Enthusiastic, Persistent and Prepared.

What I strive to bring to the table as a franchisor is my mentorship, passion, support and leadership. I admit that I don't know it all and I am willing to learn. I take others' ideas and perspectives into consideration. Some of the best practices in my business have come from my franchises and staff. I listen when a franchisee, staff member or consultant has an idea or needs my ear, and if they are not bending my ear I need to bend theirs to keep the communication ongoing. When the company was honoured with a Canadian Franchise Association's Franchise Choice Designation Award in 2012, it really touched my heart because that comes directly from the franchisees. At the end of the day their success and happiness is what I strive for and what keeps the business thriving.

My vision for growing Lice Squad Canada is to continue to promote the brand and the good work that we do. I am humbled to have the moniker "The Nice Lice Squad Lady". It may not be glamorous but it has afforded a great deal of relief to many people. I enjoy the puns, the variety of work, and all of the great people I meet and work with. My ultimate goal is to continue to attract quality partners and staff and to see the remaining Canadian territories serviced within five years.

My advice for those who want to understand franchising better is to investigate the Canadian Franchise Association. This trade association is a valuable resource. In these tough economic times it is important to celebrate franchising in Canada and encourage others to support the Canadian franchise industry because we all benefit from franchising in one way or another. I read a statistic that said 40% of our work force is employed through franchising. That is impressive. Imagine if our youth, who are crucial to the success of this country, took their entrepreneurial ideas and grew them through franchising!

I love what I do for a living. Life is precious and I am grateful to be using my time in the most meaningful and fulfilling ways. I was fortunate to realize early in my career that it was not all about me or the bottom line. I chose to create a balanced approach instead of striving and getting stuck in the workaholic lifestyle, and I grew at my own pace. I will never have the regret of missing out on my children's daily lives or not having the time to do what really matters most to me. That is what I classify as success. It is not about the external things like money, titles or pedigrees. It comes from a deeper place. It is about balance and the quality of my life and what that brings to the lives of others. Success is feeling completely content with who I am and where I am despite external circumstances.

Franchising has provided me balance and a quality of life that I was looking for. It allowed me to tap into the power of numbers. I do not go it alone.

My advice to my own children or anyone who cares to ask for it is to surround yourself with love and positivity. Never lose sight of your inner child and make time to play. Don't let success change you but rather share what you have been blessed with and support others in the pursuit of their happiness, success and dreams. Simply put, treat others as you wish to be treated, and spread joy.

When you start something you never know where it will take you, but you will never know until you start. I encourage you to start something great today. Your idea or action could very well be the next big thing that changes your life or someone else's life for the better and ultimately makes you one great Canadian.

Dawn Mucci

Founder

Dawn Mucci is a mother, entrepreneur, franchisor, writer, singer, published author and corporate citizen who is passionate about life and business. She has been recognized for creating a unique franchise concept with her company Lice Squad Canada and continues to contribute and give back to the franchise industry and her community by sitting on the Board of Directors for the Canadian Franchise Association, the Economic Development Advisory Council for Innisfil, the Board of Directors for the Children's Aid Foundation of Simcoe County and is a member of the Life Saving Society of Canada.

Her real world experience in business has given her a unique perspective and a creative enthusiasm which she shares through her creative writing and other professional endeavours. A natural storyteller, she is inspired by the stories of others and loves to share and celebrate the accomplishments of fellow Canadians.

Lice Squad Canada Inc.
3A King Street South
Cookstown, ON L0L 1L0

Phone: 888-LICE-SQUAD (542-3778)
Fax: 705-458-8887
Email: help@licesquad.com
Website: www.licesquad.com

CHAPTER 8

Nerds On Site

"We don't service technology... we serve people with technology."

Nerds On Site delivers complete technology hardware, software and service solutions to small/medium enterprises (SMEs), single office/home offices (SOHOs), corporations and individuals, on five continents. Their red shirted *entrepre*NERDS can be spotted driving little red NerdMobiles in 10 countries worldwide.

And it all started last century (1995) with John & David...

John Harbarenko and David Redekop worked at FutureShop, a great Canadian retail operation, in London, Ontario. John was in the tech service department and David in tech sales. John spotted a clear and definite need before too long. "I really felt for all of these people who came in for computer service. They would start out by separating and unplugging the wires, next they had to disassemble their equipment, then pack it in a protected manner and stow it away safely in their car. After driving to a computer 'doctor' and parking, they still had to figure out how to get a heavy and awkward sized package into the shop and pray that the lines wouldn't be too long before reaching the service depot. When they finally got the call that their computer was fixed, they had to go through the entire process in reverse once again. Hopefully, it was only a one time fiasco, but what if the computer still wasn't fixed?"

The need for the computer doctor to go to the client and provide focused and personalized care was obvious. To test the waters he placed an ad in the local Penny-Saver and had 28 calls the first day! Scrambling on evenings and weekends he began answering those cries for help. It wasn't long before David took notice of his bud's enterprising efforts and asked if he needed a partner. He did.

Fueled by passion – and credit cards – they took the leap of faith and left their jobs. And so was born Nerds On Site! In five short years they had built a solid brand and reputation rippling out from London and the surrounding area with more than a dozen nerds on their growing team. Blair, their friend and co-worker at their previous employer, joined the team early on and was instrumental in helping build that reputation. Today he's still referred to as *super*Nerd – the first nerd.

Charlie Regan used to buy computers from David at FutureShop. Once Nerds On Site started up he'd stop in every now and then with coffee and donuts to say hi. "From the beginning they were crazy in love with their work. And what a great name – Nerds On Site – it's a strong marketing message itself!" In early 2001 he threw in with John and David, but it still took more than three years before they put any kind of partnership agreement on paper. "We knew and liked each other, trusted each other as well, but frankly we were just far too busy to worry about paper of that sort early on".

Moving away from the traditional employer/employee model was instrumental to building out Nerds On Site (NOS) at this time. NOS V2 – as it's referred to now – introduced the Independent Contractor business model incorporating Rules of

Engagement and the CHARGE values system. NOS's client philosophy and culture is defined and articulated with three levels of Rules of Engagement (RofE).

The first level (and most important) is the eNerd to client RofE. This defines exactly how they agree to treat their clients – even to the level of removing shoes at the door of any home servicing. Next is eNerd to eNerd RofE which defines how eNerds work together as project team members and professionals. "Authorship equates to ownership" as the saying goes, so these RofE's are written and edited by eNerds worldwide, reflecting unique cultural elements of each region NOS operates in.

The third level of these is eNerd to NOS/NOS to eNerd RofE's – written by John, David and Charlie to articulate how the company will work with their enterprise contractors and likewise eNerds with NOS. The *CHARGE* values define both the character they look for in new eNerd applicants and works on developing further as they build out their own enterprises under the umbrella of the international brand.

C – Confident & Competent CEOs (Capability Expansion Orchestrators)

H – Honest Human Engineers

A – Attitudes of Humility

R – Responsive & Resourceful

G – Goal & Destination Focused

E – Engaging & Enthusiastic!

A key question we ask our potential contractors is the best indicator of an eNerd's suitability for our independent contractor model. "What have you learned about customer service?" The candidates who show us that they have an appreciation for good customer service and are willing to go the extra mile when necessary are clearly winners from the start. We would highly recommend to anyone and everyone who is thinking of running their own business to ask this question of themselves, and those with whom they intend to work.

Work on creating an enterprise wide collaboration and control system began in earnest as well at this time (IamANerd – IAAN). With IAAN, Canada-wide and international expansion could be facilitated and managed. We consider IAAN our number one stealth asset. It is a full-blown ERP built from the ground up with enterprising SMEs in mind. It provides updates every 400 milliseconds on all aspects of our team, clients and markets. As a sharing vehicle it allows our successes, missteps and lessons learned to enhance client offerings and solutions daily.

The University of NERDology is also incorporated in IAAN. It feeds our worldwide team with leading edge product knowledge and *better in class* client solutions and service processes. Our UofN professors conduct internal certification programs seven days a week. An eNerd can work anywhere in the world where Nerds On Site operates. Nerd exchanges are welcomed and encouraged to enable better communications and understanding between team members and even cultures.

OUR MISSION:

To circle the world passionately driving up the Pleasure, Productivity and Profitability (3Ps) of technology in the lives of our Clients... and have fun doing so!

OUR VISION:

Nerds On Site works to make itself a more enjoyable and effective partner of choice for clients everywhere. Our constant and passionate pursuit of the 3Ps in their workplaces and homes generates more raving fans each and every day! What we do and how we do it, contributes meaningfully to an ever more engaged, empowered, enterprising, and sharing world.

www.NerdsOnSite.com

www.iWanttobeaNerd.com

www.SME.NerdsOnSite.com

www.FilltheBeetleFeedthePeople.com

www.MYbusinessOS.com

www.RAFenterprising.com

David Redekop

Co-Founder

For as long as he can remember, David has had a passion for technology, especially in how it can improve our lives and businesses. As a co-founder of Nerds On Site, David has enjoyed the challenges of its history in many aspects, including growth and expansion – both personally and professionally.

David has lived in various countries around the world, including Bolivia and South Africa and benefited tremendously from those cultural integrations. He believes that Entrepreneurialism and Free Enterprise are at the core of economic growth and the future of our next generation. Education must adapt and reform to the new realities of the connected world, borderless commerce and ease of trade.

David was born in a Mennonite colony in Mexico, immigrated to Canada at the age of 15 and speaks 4.5 languages. He is married and has four young sons, with high expectations to change the world we live in.

Charles D. Regan

Owner and CEO

Charlie is an owner and CEO (capability expansion orchestrator) of a number of reasonably interesting and growing enterprises – Nerds On Site, Tactical Marketing Solutions, Augusta Business Coaching, One Extra Guy, among others. He also works closely with several more Canadian and American based firms.

He is a founding Executive Board Member for the Central Business District of Detroit and the Greater Detroit and Windsor Japan-America Society.

Charlie guest lectured for a number of years at the University of Windsor as part of their Co-Op Master of Business Administration (M.B.A.) program, as well as the University of Michigan.

Business operations around the world, coaching, as well as speaking engagements, have put Charlie in direct contact with a wide range of operations in the service, manufacturing, government, retail, and educational sectors. His general focus remains the **value** as well as the **responsibility** of the "enterprising entrepreneurial" contribution to both individual organizations and the global community at large.

Originally from Ottawa, Canada, he and his wife Jackie today reside in Lakeshore, Ontario and are parents to four adult children.

John Harbarenko

Co-Founder

In 1995, John was working as a computer technician at an electronics big-box store when he saw a need in the marketplace for 'personalized' technology service, and an opportunity to break the ice between computer owners, and computer nerds. That same year, he and David Redekop co-founded Nerds On Site to fill this void in the market and provide onsite services to homes and businesses.

A peacemaker at heart, John strives to understand all sides of any equation, and has what some might consider an over-zealous dedication to finding humour amongst ordinary (or even tense) landscapes.

Exceeding a passion for technology in and of itself, is John's fanaticism for exploring all of the possible impacts of technology across the many facets of life.

John was born in Alberta, Canada, and currently resides in Ontario with his wife and three children.

Collectively, John and David (Redekop) speak a total of 4.6 languages.

Nerds On Site Inc.

131 Wharncliffe Road South
Third Floor
London ON N6J 2K4
CANADA

Phone: 877-696-3737 (877-MYNERDS)
Email: info@nerdsonsite.com
Website: www.nerdsonsite.com

CHAPTER 9

Coffee Culture Café & Eatery

Come for the taste, stay for a visit.

Every time you stop at a coffee shop, you are stepping into a long history, since coffee houses have been around for hundreds of years on every continent of our planet. Although each geographical location has its own cultural flair, the commonality they all share is that coffeehouses serve as informal, social, artistic and intellectual centres. They are places for people of all classes to congregate, talk, write, entertain friends, gossip, make business deals, attend lectures, catch up on news, and argue politics.

The popularity of coffee and the formation of the European coffee house culture dates back to the 16th century, not too long after Pope Clement VIII declared, "This devil's drink is so delicious...we should cheat the devil by baptizing it". So he did! The baptized coffee became acclaimed for being a sobering rather than an intoxicating drink that "stimulates mental activity and heightens perceptions rather than dulling the senses". The Pope also added that it would be a shame for only the criminals to enjoy this delicious drink. Today, coffee is the most popular drink in the world, and it is estimated that people around the world consume more than two billion cups a day. It is also second only to oil in its ranking as the largest traded commodity in the world. However, that was not the reason we developed Coffee Culture Café & Eatery.

Coffee Culture was created as a result of the enjoyable experiences I shared with friends and family at some of the traditional European cafés. The void we spotted in the marketplace became apparent to me when we didn't have equivalent places to enjoy. I realized that the drastic difference between the Canadian and European coffee houses is that in Canada, other than going to a bar or to someone's home, there is really no place for people to gather for an extended period of time for conversation and relaxation. We started Coffee Culture Café & Eatery because we saw the opportunity and the need for a European-style café in Canada, although for our European café, we decided to add a larger variety of tasty and fresh foods to the theme.

Our goal at Coffee Culture was to cater to and encourage people of all walks of life and all ages to come and hang out.

Once we went to work on the concept, the name was developed with the assistance of long-term colleagues and a marketing company. When Coffee Culture opened its first location in 2006, we found ourselves expanding rather quickly. You can only imagine our elation as we watched Canadians embrace Coffee Culture and this old European tradition. We wanted our customers to know that it's okay to "Come for the taste and stay for a visit!"

There is a saying "Man does not live on coffee alone, so eat a pastry!" Just the mouth-watering thought of a fresh, home-baked muffin or baked goods is enough to nurture a soul. That is why our commitment to the quality and freshness of the food we serve exceeds any of our competitors' standards. Whether our competitors purchase standard pre-packaged products or have a central kitchen preparing and distributing their goods to them, they cannot possibly compete with the freshness of our in-house bakery. At Coffee Culture, our staff arrives at 5 a.m. They begin by warming the ovens as they prepare to bake all sorts of fresh gourmet foods: breakfast bagels, muffins and an assortment of European pastries that are fresh and ready at 6:30 a.m. when we open our doors. As our name suggests, we also purchase high quality, whole roasted coffee beans and have them blended and roasted to our specifications to ensure each freshly brewed cup of coffee, espresso, latte and cappuccino, is deliciously satisfying. Our lunch and late night offerings include grilled sandwiches, soups and various house specialties. You also cannot go wrong with our late night decadent desserts.

One thing you can always depend on at Coffee Culture is great quality, delicious tasting food, comfortable seating in a warm relaxing atmosphere and great service. What's not to love?

I have always been determined and motivated to help people excel and to make a difference in their lives. Starting out in restaurants and working my way from the bottom up in the hospitality business, I learned that hard work was the only way to create opportunities in life. From the beginning stages of my working days, which provided me with a vast education in full service kitchen experience, I understood that the kitchen and the food that comes out of it are the heart of any restaurant and certainly the heart of our business. Many people have dreams of owning their own business, especially restaurants, but they don't have the know-how or the hands-on experience to do it on their own. I wanted to help people who didn't have previous business experience in the hospitality industry and watch them enjoy success.

The restaurant business has one of the largest failure rates in the business world; however, with a good system and with experienced knowledge, we can help people succeed. To ensure the operator's success, I always stress the importance of managing a restaurant well and understanding the business and customer's needs. The best teacher is example, and I wanted to put together and share the success of a system and the concepts that I believed in. Franchising was the perfect career for me since it is all about building relationships, meeting new people, seeing people succeed and helping people meet and share their dreams.

The fastest way I know to help others achieve success in their professional and personal lives is by franchising a concept. For us, potentially good franchisees would be hard working individuals with good character, people that care for their business and are willing to be successful. To me, their past history speaks volumes by demonstrating their past life habits and patterns. They must possess the ability to manage a number of people and finances successfully. They must be willing and able to commit to a full-time, hands-on, day-to-day involvement in overseeing the operations of their franchise and to mentor and train their employees. They need to have the ability to motivate the employees to deliver an exceptional customer experience every time; this is of utmost importance to us.

Devcor Developments is our real estate development holdings company and our team that is always seeking and purchasing new real estate to help expand our brands. A franchisee does not need to go out and find a site to build on. Instead they can help by steering us to some possible sites in their desired neighbourhood. Our development team then goes behind the scenes to find the potential locations. Whether a franchisee is looking to open in a big city, in the suburbs, in downtown, or even a smaller more quaint location, we may already have the perfect real estate site available.

We make sure our franchisees feel supported every step of the way. Obsidian Group Inc. is our management company, formed in 1996 to develop, market and manage hospitality interests. They manage our three franchise systems: Crabby Joe's Tap & Grill, Coffee Culture Café & Eatery and Union Burger. Obsidian Group Inc. is made up of a very impressive group of management and hospitality professionals. It is one of the fastest growing and most progressive hospitality companies in Canada today. Obsidian Group Inc. incorporates experienced management personnel in operations, human resources, marketing, real estate, construction, accounting, franchise, culinary arts, etc. These are all hands-on, hard-working, dedicated individuals, who have an entrepreneurial background and share a common vision of success. These amazing experts are available at all times to provide our franchisees with all the necessary tools, training, and mentoring; they can address any concerns a franchisee might have in every aspect of their business. We also believe that it is important to provide the franchisee with the opportunity to purchase the building in which they operate their specific stores and offer non-traditional opportunities for the right candidates. So you see, just as the franchisee is investing in us, we are investing in them. Once they become a part of our franchise family, we will do whatever it takes to assist them in succeeding both in their business and their personal lives.

Studies have proven that not only does the aroma of brewed coffee cause pleasure, coffee also has powerful antioxidant properties that neutralize free radicals in our bodies and thereby protect the body's cells from damage caused by stress. After we actually take a sip of this tantalizing brew, we are infused with a sense of well-being, feeling both relaxed and invigorated, exhilarated yet clearheaded. Anyone who has traveled will recognize that Coffee Culture is designed as an Old World style café, where customers make it a frequent destination for conversation and relaxation. It is the perfect spot to grab a quiet cup of coffee, hold a casual business meeting, or take advantage of the café's wireless Internet access and plasma TV. Weather permitting of course, a few sidewalk tables lend a Euro flair to boot. Coffee Culture aims to be your neighbourhood meeting place where we cater to all of your senses. Your senses don't lie. Just ask them. They will tell you that they can't get enough of our delicious tastes, warm relaxing atmosphere, comfortable seating, great service and fabulous aromas.

Gus Karamountzos

Founder

Gus Karamountzos was born in Karya, Greece on October 2, 1960. He was the youngest of three children, the oldest a sister and the middle child a brother. He was raised in a small village in extreme poverty. Gus' father was a farmer, and his mother helped out where she could along with all of her household chores. When Gus was 10, the family moved to a bigger town with a population of 35,000. There the family was able to start a new way of life and were fortunate to take advantage of the education that was available to them at the time.

In 1977 at 17 years old, Gus was encouraged by his parents, but especially his father, to join his brother in Canada in an attempt to make an even better life for himself. His father knew that there would be more opportunities in Canada and he wanted the brothers to reunite. Although he left behind a lot of family members, including his father, mother and sister, Gus ventured into the world to create a new and better life for himself.

Gus immigrated to Stratford, Ontario where he joined his older brother, along with a

few distant relatives who had left Greece before he did. He worked in restaurants in odd jobs in the kitchen and as a cook. He met Helen, a beautiful Greek woman, whom he married in 1982 in Toronto, where she lived and had just graduated from Ryerson University. In 1983, they celebrated the birth of their first son, Peter. In 1984, a second son George was born and in 1988 his daughter, Tina, joined the family too.

While raising his family, Gus put all his efforts into working and building equity so that he would be able to survive and raise a family. Helen mostly stayed home raising the children along with help from the children's grandparents, and she helped Gus as much as possible in the family-operated restaurant. Gus continued to open individually operated restaurants. With his experience, his passion for food and cooking, and his experience operating the kitchens, he was able to operate each of the restaurants and made enough to provide for his family. It was his passion for the restaurant business, his commitment, drive and perfectionism that led Gus into many business opportunities, including Crabby Joe's Tap & Grill, Coffee Culture Café & Eatery, and Union Burger.

As the years went by, after many sacrifices and relocations, Gus and his family made the Greater Toronto Area their home and business headquarters, which today manages and operates more than 250 properties and restaurant locations throughout Canada and the United States.

Coffee Culture Café & Eatery

2556 Meadowpine Blvd.
Mississauga, ON L5N 6P9

Phone: 905-813-8030
Email: info@coffeeculturecafe.com
Website: http://www.coffeeculturecafe.com/

CHAPTER 10

Pizza Nova

PIZZA NOVA®

"We strive to exceed our customer's expectations each and every time!"

Although pizza has been around for over 3,000 years, it wasn't until the discovery of tomatoes by the Spanish in the 1500s, combined with the invention of mozzarella cheese in Italy three centuries later, that Italian pizza as we know it today was created.

In 1963, our goal was to start a business that shared an authentic part of our heritage with our community. When my three brothers and I started Pizza Nova, pizza was not a common or popular food item. In fact, it was considered a snack to be eaten between meals. Just as pizza has evolved through the years, so has Pizza Nova evolved from the little place we opened in Scarborough, Ontario back in 1963. Although it is still a family operated business, I am now the sole owner and CEO of Pizza Nova, and my son Domenic is the President. In 1969 our first franchisee joined the Pizza Nova family. Since then we've expanded the Pizza Nova brand with over 130 locations across southern Ontario. Today, we serve over four million pizzas annually with a choice of 30 toppings, along with a wide range of other menu items. In 2004, we changed our logo and design to enhance our brand, made operational changes, and continued to nurture and grow our franchise family. Throughout, the one thing that has absolutely stayed the same is our original commitment to authenticity, consistency, quality, cleanliness and service.

Authenticity demands consistency, consistency demands good quality, good quality demands cleanliness, and all of them together require good customer service, especially in a niche market! That is why we have created an experience rather than just another restaurant. We are not just another pizza joint located in a mall or plaza, or one of the strip stores that you happen to see from the highway. We want people to come in because we are a community pizza place. We really enjoy cultivating a great customer base, for they are the backbone of our business. They know they can depend on the fact that we will always provide a consistently high quality product, served in an authentic Italian environment. Through the years, we have never changed our recipes or the ingredients we use in preparing them, so that they become a kind of comfort food. This is specifically to assure that the same familiarity and quality that the customer has come to love is what they will get each and every time. At the same time however, we are always on the lookout for new and authentic ways to enhance their experience even more.

Recently, after travelling back and forth from Bari, Italy to Toronto, coupled with extensive training and approval by the Bari Consortium, Pizza Nova was awarded the exclusive rights to serve to Canadians the protected Focaccia Barese™. Focaccia Barese™ (pronounced "fo'kkat-cha ba'reezeh") is a particular type of oven-baked Italian bread that is related to the pizza base, though it is definitely not the same. Focaccia Barese™ was made famous by the people of Bari in the 1800s and it is an honoured and protected recipe that is prepared in a traditional method with precise ingredients of specific quality. The recipe itself is an IGP product (Indicazione Geografica Protetta - Protected Geographic Indication), which means it is protected by the European "stamp of approval" that guards the reputation and quality of regional foods. Pizza Nova has earned the honour and privilege of carrying on the tradition of this protected recipe here in Canada, and we are ever so proud of it!

Through the years we've learned that quality control is the key to never wavering from our motto! At first, for example, we bought Swift Pepperoni, from a U.S. company that made the best pepperoni to be found. In time, the Swift Company was sold, and then it was sold again. Realizing that our reputation was too dependent on other people, we decided to become self-sufficient in order to assure the consistency and quality of our product. The solution was to have our own pepperoni recipe produced for us.

Another example of our striving for premium quality is our bacon. Most pizza places are not as particular as we are in their choice of bacon; however, due to the fat content we do not use the end cuts of bacon at Pizza Nova. After finding the best brand of bacon on the market, even though it's very costly, we negotiated to purchase only the centre cut of the bacon. This product is prepared and packed for us according to our specifications.

Another way we ensure the quality of excellence is exemplified in the picking of the tomatoes we use. We have flown to California numerous times in order to ensure that the tomatoes specifically packed for us are the best of the crop. The automatic pickers have technology that allows them to determine the tomatoes' level of ripeness as they are picked. They also discard the tomatoes that are not up to our standards. Within six hours of being picked the tomatoes are canned in an olive oil-lined can that contains a manually placed basil leaf. The tomatoes we use for our sauces are vine-ripened on the plant and are the most expensive tomatoes purchased on the market, but money is not what drives us. The quality we provide does!

When I was 23, I managed 125 women at a sewing plant. On the average we produced 1,350 pieces of children's wear daily. Although I was a quick learner, when I was young I did not have much of a formal education. I learned a lot from my life experiences. Every day I find myself being forever grateful for (and always using) the gift of common sense that God bestowed upon me. One of the skills I acquired as a manager, though, was the ability to work with and read people. So it was no surprise when I found my calling in 1969 with our first attempt at franchising. It is the perfect career for a person like me who loves people. I love to help people, especially the ones who really want to be helped. At first, when an employee wanted to start a Pizza Nova of his own, it didn't really work out too well. There were control issues to be dealt with; we had to figure out how to make it work, and we really didn't know what we were doing or what to pay the people involved. In time we learned that a franchisee is a person who wants to be in his own business, but needs a little guidance. So we provided management and guidance, and together we grew.

In actuality, we were more interested in the people that wanted to work for us than building the franchise itself. If we liked the person and they showed potential, even if they didn't have enough money to invest, we helped them get their start. We have a lot of franchises who were pizza makers and even drivers at some of our stores, and they are terrific people. They were excited about our product, worked hard, loved people, and were dependable. All these people needed was a hand, and we were happy to provide it. Those franchises are successful business owners today, and they are still with Pizza Nova. We really wanted the right franchises, and we invested in building the company from the ground up with a good foundation of hard-working, worthwhile people. I would still do the same today for the right franchisee, though in today's market it's a little different. People want to be in the pizza business but they don't know anything about the business, so they come to us and we have to show them everything from A to Z. Back then, it was usually an experienced pizza maker that was looking for a break. We can show someone how to make a pizza, but you cannot teach someone people skills. You cannot teach someone how to be likable or how to bring back a first, second or third time customer. Natural abilities can go a long way!

I can tell you that we've had our ups and downs along the way, since success never happens without some failure. The key is to learn from your mistakes and to trust yourself. At times a decision may seem like a mistake to others, but you must learn when to trust your gut feeling. One of those times was just a few years ago when, after 40 years of being in business, we decided to align our image with our brand. My son and I were the only ones that kept insisting that our store design and logo was not in harmony with the brand image. We wanted to be the Starbucks of pizza. We knew our product was definitely a high end product but our look was not. My wife Gemma, who has been my strongest supporter through the years, profoundly disagreed with us, and so did everyone else. Against all the opposition, we decided to move forward with our plan and hired a very well-known firm to synchronize our brand representation. They embraced this idea as well. We continued to follow our gut feeling against all odds because somewhere inside we knew that it was the right time for the next step we needed to take. In the end, when all was said and done, instead of failing we prevailed! The results were exhilarating as we saw our old customers returning and liking the changes. Our client base grew and so did our bottom line, at all of our locations.

It has been enormously heartwarming to receive all the awards, accolades and recognition through the years. I would have to say, that when it comes to the awards, my biggest thrill was in receiving the Canadian Franchise Association (CFA) Franchise of the Year Award, 2012. Getting recognition from my peers and colleagues for all our hard work and being number one among all the amazing franchises Canada has to offer certainly tugged at my heartstrings.

The other enormous reward I got was by being of service to others. As a positive and upbeat man, I want to surround myself with positive people and do not like or tolerate drama and gossip. Just as we care about our customers' satisfaction, we definitely want our employees and franchisees to be content too. We are constantly on the lookout for innovative ways to support them also. Among other benefits, one of the things we did a few years back was to hire a full-time clinical psychologist onsite at our support office. All an employee or franchisee needs to do is pick up the phone and set up a free appointment. We never know who sees her and we don't need to. We just want to ensure that our people are equipped with the tools they need to be at peace. I carry a cell phone that is only accessible to my franchisees. They know I am available 24/7… but the phone never rings.

On a personal level we choose to serve our community and society by giving to a handful of charities that we believe in: Variety Village, seniors, battered women, sick children and drug rehabilitation. In business, as in life, being of service to others is an honour and a privilege. Being of service comes with great rewards and blessings that are not attainable in any other way. It's kind of like a Catch-22, since a person who is happy with himself or herself is happy to serve others. A person who serves others cannot feel bad inside. A person who does not feel bad inside cannot hurt another. A person who is kind and considerate attracts people like moths to a light. Our goal is to be the light and to help others get there too! You don't have to start big. For starters, just give someone a smile.

Sam Primucci

Founder

Sam Primucci was born in Palazzo San Gervasio, in the region of Basilicata, Italy. He immigrated to Canada in 1952. In 1963, he and his brothers opened a small pizzeria called Pizza Nova on the corner of Lawrence and Kennedy in Toronto. From those humble beginnings, it has grown to be what it is today, with over 130 locations across Ontario. The spirit, ambition and courage that it took to go from being a new immigrant to creating what Pizza Nova is today has not only continued to fuel the company's success, but has served as an inspiration to many new entrepreneurial candidates in this country.

Just as Pizza Nova began and succeeds as a family business, Sam recognizes his greatest success is his marriage to his wife Gemma, raising his two sons Domenic and Michael, his daughters-in-law Anna and Loredanna, and his four grandchildren, Lucas, Samuel, Gemma and Mara.

Sam has been President of the CNE Food Products Association for 12 years; he has also been honoured for Business Excellence by the Italian Chamber of Commerce, the Canadian Italian Business and Professional Association, CAFE, CARITAS and has won the 2012 Canadian Franchise Association Franchisee of the Year Award.

In addition to his professional success, M. Primucci belongs to the Military Order of St. Agatha of Paterno, is a knight of Malta, Cavaliere Al Merito Della Repubblica Italiana, as well as a member of the Associazione Nazionale della Polizia di Stato.

His professional experience has enabled him to contribute to the success of his community volunteer activities. He is past president of the Italian Canadians for Progress, serves on the Finance Committee for the Epiphany of Our Lord Parish, is past Chairman of the Epiphany Soccer League, and is an Honorary Member of the Victoria Park Recreation Centre.

Under the direction of M. Sam Primucci, Pizza Nova continues to be a double digit-growth organization that has been awarded multiple awards and accolades for its achievements in growth, packaging, branding, and media. Pizza Nova also continues to outshine its competition in its commitment and support of charitable organizations and events within and beyond the community it serves.

Pizza Nova

Support Office
2247 Midland Avenue
Toronto, Ontario
Canada, M1P 4R1

Phone: 416-439-0051
Email: info@pizzanova.com
Website: www.pizzanova.com

CHAPTER 11

PropertyGuys.com

"If you think you can do a thing or, if you think you can't do a thing, you're right! — Henry Ford"

Some people are destined for success. Others achieve it because they are lucky enough to find a vision they believe in and are determined to make it a reality. It is said that most business success stories are a result of regular people finding a void in the market and creating an appealing solution. My partners and I recognized just such an opportunity in the real estate market. With a lot of hard work and a little bit of luck, we have built a big idea into a successful franchise organization.

It wasn't that long ago that the real estate market was monopolized by brokers and agents. As a buyer or seller, there was simply no other option than engaging a real estate agent. They were the only ones who had access to inside information about listings and how to market a home. In the end, whether you wanted to or not, you paid a hefty commission fee that substantially reduced your net selling price once your house sold.

Initially, we didn't go looking for what would turn out to be a lifelong career. One of my partners and I were full-time business students in Moncton, New Brunswick, when we just happened to notice a lot of orange and black "For Sale by Owner" signs on lawns. It struck us that lots of people were trying to bypass the high cost of agent commissions but they didn't have the tools to do it very well. We also realized that a great "place" to organize independent home sellers would be this new phenomenon called "the Internet." We saw an opportunity in the market to arrange listing data and package it for these sellers in our community. We knew we could help, so we did.

We put all the necessary components for selling a house under one roof, so to speak, and were able to simplify the process for selling without an agent in our community. With our new program, sellers no longer had to waste their time and energy accumulating everything they needed to sell their own house. We created a central location online for their information, making it easy for potential buyers to peruse their listing with just a few clicks of a mouse.

A key reason why PropertyGuys.com is where it is today was the expansion of our partnership from two to four very early in our development. While many partnerships can struggle, or even fail, ours has been very stable and a key element in our success. Jeremy Demont and I started PropertyGuys.com in 1998, and Dale Betts and Walter Melanson joined the team in 1999. The four of us are still partners today and serve as the executives of the company.

What has allowed this partnership to thrive is that we all have different skills and experience but we make our business decisions as a team. Integral to our success is that we share a common vision and we are united in our efforts to achieve that goal. In addition, the four of us push each other to excel at our distinct roles in the organization. All of us are proud of our ownership and involvement in the growth of the company.

PropertyGuys.com was launched as a service that brings together home sellers and buyers, online and on the ground. Our website provides a proprietary environment where they interact with each other directly. In other words, we are able to empower sellers and buyers to connect by eliminating the need for a traditional real estate agent in the process. The program we developed gives home sellers the tools and training to sell their home themselves for a reasonable flat fee, eliminating the need to pay a high percentage of the value of their home in agent commissions.

My background and my passion has always been in real estate and franchising. We were rather green, both in age and in business experience, when we started PropertyGuys.com. Once we were successful with our business in the Moncton market, we wanted to expand our program. Franchising seemed like the right business model to use because it would enable like-minded individuals to open up new markets and use the technology we had developed. Our lower start-up capital investment relative to other franchise opportunities made it attractive to prospective franchises.

In 2002 we sold our first franchise. In fact, we had incredible momentum at that time and sold one franchise per month for 10 months straight. It was an extremely busy period, and we had to manoeuvre around any bumps we encountered along that steep learning curve without slowing down. Three years later, we were selling a franchise a week, and three years after that, we celebrated the sale of our 100th franchise.

As we grew our network, we continued to find ways to keep overheads low by applying innovative thinking to minimize expenditures. For example, our first lawn signs were recycled. When the voting polls closed in our municipal election, we approached the city and offered to remove the corrugated plastic election lawn signs that were found all over the streets if we could keep the signs as compensation. The city was happy to oblige, and we were able to reprint our signs at a low cost.

In our excitement to build the franchise network, we were also learning what type of individual best fit our brand and our goals. Over time, we massaged our recruiting and screening process to help us get better at awarding franchises. There are times when addressing oversights can result in a better process. Today, the franchises in our network complete a profile screening as part of the award process. They all take great pride in servicing their customers and share their clients' excitement over the money saved when they sell their home.

We also were not afraid to reach for outside guidance when we needed it. Recognizing that we had a lot to learn about branding, for example, we engaged a great outside resource to help position the brand. There came a point in our relationship with Roy Williams and the Wizard Academy when we realized we needed to make a bold statement about how different we were from the traditional real estate industry. In 2008 our distinctive round sign was born. When we launched the new design to our franchises on a cruise ship in the Caribbean, you could literally feel us shift as a cohesive team to a higher level of brand clarity. It was an unparalleled moment in the history of our company.

Through the years we became known as market leaders and developed a great reputation for breaking the mold in the industry. We continue to lead through innovation and are constantly upgrading our web platform and our portfolio of services to ensure that we offer our customers an appealing and easy-to-use service. To be a successful operator in our franchise system, you need to enjoy helping people. We definitely look for extroverts – people that are energetic and outgoing and can build teams with those same qualities. We also seek out individuals who have lots of drive or some entrepreneurial experience, and an interest in real estate.

Today we are proud to say that we have a great reputation with our customers and our franchises. There are over 120 PropertyGuys.com franchises serving over 600 communities across Canada, and we are still growing. We have thousands of active listings on our website and tens of thousands of visitors each day, with still more opportunities to bring our brand to more Canadian communities.

The most common question I get asked by budding franchisors is how to initiate the franchising process. My response is that they will first need to evaluate the franchise potential of their business by answering four key questions.

Question #1: Is the business concept franchise-able? Sure, "franchise-able" may not be a word, but it is an important notion to understand. You need to look at the concept objectively and identify the systems that would be required to support a network of franchises.

Question #2: Will the concept appeal to the local, national or global market? Will it work in a variety of locations and economic conditions?

Question #3: Is the concept a fad that may fade in a few years, or does it have long term sustainability?

Question #4: Is there a specific skill that's required to do the job, and can you train people to do it?

You will also need to learn how to replicate your success or basically, clone yourself. To do that, take the time to record every detail of your day from the moment you wake up until the time you go to bed at night. This will provide the foundation of your future franchise blueprint, the Operations Manual. Establishing procedures and an operational backbone is the most vital component in franchising since – in addition to your intellectual property, including your brand and your logo – that is essentially what you are selling.

Once you are confident that your business suits a franchise model, you will need to formulate franchise projections and test various financial scenarios. You will need to be able to clearly articulate how your business works so your prospective franchises will be able to project their own path to success. Only then should you decide if you are willing and able to initiate franchising.

We are still the only franchise network in Canada that provides a marketing program for home sellers in the real estate industry. Although there are other "for sale by owner" companies, not one of them is a franchise system. We believe the PropertyGuys.com proprietary platform plus franchise network gives us that winning combination of national and local, virtual and personal.

Truthfully, I don't believe franchising is for everybody. In my case, it has been a lot of hard work. I was fortunate enough to do it with a dedicated team of partners. I was also lucky to have a great support system at home as well. I was taught early in life that "the benefit of entrepreneurship is that what you put into your business is exactly what you receive in return," so giving up on my personal dream was never an option.

You can make your dream of franchising come true too. There is such a range of franchise concepts out there that could scratch your itch – whether you're a left-brain accountant or an outdoorsman. What is most important is that you find the right fit for you! When you do, you will find that the franchise world can be challenging and fulfilling on the personal and financial levels. You just have to find your niche and recognize that you too, with a lot of hard work, can be one of the lucky ones!

Ken LeBlanc

President and CEO

Ken LeBlanc, president and CEO of PropertyGuys.com has for the past 15 years, been turning seeds of dreams into fields of plenty... plenty of success that is! The modern day "dream weaver" was awarded the Business Development Bank of Canada (BDC) Young Entrepreneur of the Year, 2002, the same year PropertyGuys.com sold their first franchise. The awards and accolades have not stopped coming in ever since.

Started in 1998 with the intention to help, PropertyGuys.com has simplified the selling process for the private sale real estate sector and revolutionized Canada's entire real estate industry forever. Today PropertyGuys.com is represented in 10 provinces and territories by over 123 franchises (and still growing), that are supporting over 600 communities and providing 350 jobs in 400 cities across Canada. Their website generates 400,000 visitors a month and consists of over 10,000 active listings.

Ken LeBlanc invests much of his time mentoring the next generation of Canadian entrepreneurs. He speaks publicly on the challenges facing youth in business and invests in inspiring the next generation. Most recently he founded YPG, a youth entrepreneurship challenge that aims at putting young people front and centre nationally when it comes to entrepreneurship in Canada.

2012 – Sponsor, The Prince's Operation Entrepreneur with CYBF and the Canadian Armed Forces

2012 – Canadian Franchise Association – Franchisee Choice Award

2011 – Canadian Franchise Association – Franchisee Choice Award

2011 – Franchise Business Review – Top 50 Franchises

2011 – G20 Youth Entrepreneurship Summit – Nice, France – Canadian Representative

2010 – G20 Youth Entrepreneurship Summit in Toronto, ON – Canadian Representative

2010 – 2nd Vice Chair – Canadian Franchise Association Board of Directors

2009 – Award of Excellence – Canadian Franchise Association

2009 – Special "Guest Dragon" on CBC Dragons' Den – YPG Live Edition

2009 – CYBF – Canadian Delegate for the Prince of Wales and the Duchess of Cornwall Royal Visit

2008 – Award of Excellence – Canadian Franchise Association

2008 – Canadian Franchise Association Board of the Directors

2008 – New Brunswick Ambassador

2007 – Ernst & Young Entrepreneur of the Year Award – Atlantic Finalist

2007 – Canadian Franchise Association Award of Excellence

2006 – Greater Moncton Chamber of Commerce Excellence Awards Finalist – Emerging Business

2006 – Ken LeBlanc – Atlantic Canada's Top-50 CEOs

2005 – Greater Moncton Chamber of Commerce – Keynote Speaker – Excellence Awards

2005 – Ken LeBlanc – Atlantic Canada's Top-50 CEOs

2005 – Canadian Youth Business Foundation (CYBF) New Brunswick Best Business Award Winner

2004 – Canadian Business Franchise Magazine "Top 25 Successful Canadian Franchises for 2004"

2004 – Nominated for Canada's Outstanding CEO of the Year

2004 – Ken LeBlanc – Atlantic Canada's Top-50 CEOs

2003 – Greater Moncton Chamber of Commerce Excellence Awards Finalist – Emerging Business

2003 – Greater Moncton Chamber of Commerce Excellence Awards Finalist – Innovation

2003 – Greater Moncton Chamber of Commerce Excellence Awards Finalist – Marketing

2003 – Finalist in the Knowledge Industry Recognition Awards

2003 – Featured in cover story on the Canadian Business Franchise Magazine

2003 – Ken LeBlanc – Atlantic Canada's Top-50 CEOs

2002 – Business Development Bank of Canada (BDC) Young Entrepreneur of the Year

---

PropertyGuys.com National Home Office

1133 St. George Boulevard
Moncton, New Brunswick
Canada E1E 4E1

Phone: 1-866-666-9744
Toll-Free: 1-855-252-6974
Website: www.PropertyGuysFranchise.com

CHAPTER 12

Oxford Learning Centre

Since 1984 OXFORD® LEARNING

> ***"If you think education is expensive, try ignorance! — Attributed to both Andy McIntyre and Derek Bok"***

Parents know that the greatest gift they can give their children is to equip them with the right tools to succeed in life. One of the most important tools parents can provide is education. It goes without saying that society has a tremendous impact on education, which in turn comes back full circle, since the results impact society. It is common knowledge that education itself is greatly influenced by a variety of societal factors which include culture, development, traditions and beliefs. Studies have shown that for every year a boy attends school, there is a 20 percent decrease in the probability that he will engage in violent activities. The studies also concluded that increasing the percentage of children attending school in low attendance areas by a mere 10 per cent lessens the likelihood of conflict in that country. At Oxford Learning Centres we believe that high quality education can be achieved by providing our students with lifelong tools such as high self-esteem, an active, agile mind, and an understanding of how to study, learn and think.

My passion for education surged when I realized that I disagreed with the current standards of teaching methodologies and educational philosophies. The founding members of Oxford Learning Centre all shared the conviction that tutoring and teaching could be done better. Private tutoring is an ancient and honourable profession (think Socrates and Aristotle) but was being treated with disrespect by the public education sector. There was a better way to teach students so they could understand and learn rather than just memorize. The group consisted of members who taught in high school and university, who wrote curricula, and who engaged in research into cognition and intelligence. That is why we started Oxford Learning in 1984. The primary goal was to teach students a different way of thinking about the process of how they learn, to equip them with confidence in their abilities, and to teach them the tools they need to be successful students for life.

The original group of professionals included educational philosophers, psychologists, teachers, professors of education, and curriculum writers. We worked with the newest cognitive science theories of learning, teaching, and assessing, including some developed by our group. Using these theories, we set about to develop a new teaching method called Interactive Coaching, a new assessment model called Dynamic Assessment, a new scope, and new sequence theories for curriculum. From this we ended up with our own curriculum that is different from any taught anywhere else on earth, and a new assessment model that measures thinking and learning potential in a dynamic context that allows us to understand why a student is struggling. This helps us develop an individual learning plan that will create permanent changes in how the student thinks and learns. It also gives us the ability to create a new curriculum that allows kids to understand what they are learning, not just memorize and repeat until mastery.

Originally, Oxford Learning Centre was not a franchise – it was a single learning centre. But as we grew and became successful, it became obvious that franchising the business and empowering others by teaching them the system was a great way to help more children. We have been blessed by our partnership system, though I believe that unless one is in a professional practice, they should enter a partnership as a last resort. Although I am sure that partnerships can work, I just don't know of any enduring partnerships that do not include family.

That being said, all our staff and franchises are our partners and important components of our franchise family. We have our differences, but the bottom line is our common denominator and unifying factor, i.e., all of us – family or not – are committed to helping parents and children. In the end, that is what gets us past any hurdles that may arise. We insist that every member of our team create and live a balanced life. Of course there are people in the office on weekends, but if they do it too often, we send them home. Work is certainly one of life's most important activities but their home life is just as important. Balance is the key to the flow of a good life and enables us to nurture ourselves so that we have more to give to others.

The franchise system is unique in that really anyone can become a successful franchisee because it is already a proven system. The only skill that people really need is the ability to follow the system and hire the right people. They do not have to be entrepreneurs or have a degree, nor do they need any special skills. However, it is important to make sure theirs is a killer idea that works flawlessly and can manifest a good profit. Once a business is successful in its first location, it is ripe for cloning into a franchise system. The key, however, is to have enough capital to carry through the slow start-up period, which is mostly made up of massive documentation of the entire operational systems process. You must also be able to mentor, support and listen. The supportive "front line" needs to be able to supply the necessary information and valuable feedback to help the franchises fine tune their businesses. The bottom line is that the franchisor is invested in the success of the franchisee; the more successful the franchisee becomes, the more successful the brand.

Although I think a good support system is important, at the same time, I believe that success comes from within. I have always felt that ambition, drive, energy, curiosity, and the unwillingness to take no for an answer or to accept defeat, are virtues needed to accomplish anything meaningful in life. You cannot have success without some failures, and having the courage to fail (and to succeed) is probably the leading factor. I know, like anyone else who has attempted anything in life, that it is all part of the process. Some of those mistakes include impatience and expecting others to live up to our standards without spending enough time helping them to understand why it would be in their best interest to do things in a specific way. One of our biggest mistakes was probably when we made an initial move into the United States without enough capital and support to do so. It cost the company a lot of heartache and money before we got it right. But we knew that we had a really great product and that it was really different from other tutoring companies. We also knew we could really make a long-lasting difference in the lives of the kids and their families. It was the belief that we could truly make a difference that motivated me then and continues to motivate me today. After all, it is not about the money; it is about the kids and their families.

Franchising is really the best of both worlds. You get to be your own boss while using a system that is proven to be successful, so you don't have to worry about striking out on your own and failing. Unlike opening your own business, there is a massive support network in place, and a vested interest in your success. When meeting with a potential franchisee, I try to find people with the same characteristics that imbue our team. They have to love working with kids and parents. It's messy, exuberant, hard to schedule, unpredictable, joyful, and simply a crazy environment, therefore flexibility is important. If they are not adaptable and don't like to "have their cheese moved," then Oxford Learning Centre is not the best fit for them. If all they want to do is make money, maybe a donut franchise or the like would be a better fit for them.

With us, a franchisee's day-to-day life is like a day at the amusement park. There is laughing, celebrating, crying, high fives, hugs, friendships, and lots of joy. It's not work, it's the best of life!

Oxford Learning Centre is about teaching children how to learn. That is why the most monumental time for me in our business was when we hit 100 franchises. It meant that we had traction and had built an incredible and viable base which provided us the capital to develop new materials and afforded us the ability to hire additional staff. Currently we have big expansion plans in the U.S., and we are slowly expanding internationally as well. With our approach, learning comes more naturally to all children.

Before long, the results will display better outcomes in academics, social interactions, physical skills, and even emotional relationships. Outcomes like these are why more than 100,000 parents believe Oxford Learning is learning for life. As we grow, we will continue to develop new materials in-house along with a curriculum that matches the growing and ever-changing needs of today's students and parents. Now that we have become the very best in the private education sector, we can focus on being the biggest as well.

Helping others discover the personal rewards of working with families and children and giving them the tools that they need to run a successful business is what our Oxford Learning Centre franchise is about. Mostly, though, it's about the number of kids and families we can help. The more help we impart, the more successful we are. For us, business success is easy to measure since it is the number of happy, successful franchises operating across Canada and internationally. We are proud to be capitalists and do not apologize for our success, since success is what we extend to others. Our business is based on integrity, honesty, and massive passion for what we do. We know that what we put into it is what we will reap, and we are all committed to going the extra mile even if it means giving more than what we are getting paid to do. Since example is the best teacher, I as the boss, must walk my talk. When you become the example of a life well lived, you find that work is not a burden – it is one of the most vital and exciting parts of life. Follow your passion and then you too, can begin your days joyously, having fun and loving life!

Nick Whitehead

President and Founder

Nick has a doctorate in epistemology – the philosophical study of learning – and has devoted his life to working with children. Based on the results obtained from various research projects on cognition and intelligence conducted by him and by various other cognitive scientists, and by working with a group of educators, he founded Oxford Learning in 1984.

He has acted as an educational resource and consultant for the federal government and has developed policies and programs that are in use in First Nation schools across Canada. Nick is also one of the authors of the 14 Transition Years Project studies commissioned by the Ontario Ministry of Education. He has worked extensively with attention deficit disorder (A.D.D.) children for the past 24 years and has developed many of the A.D.D. educational and cognitive development programs being used in the Oxford Learning Centres.

Nick Whitehead has authored three books: *Learning to Listen: A CAP Handbook for Parents and Teachers, Will You Please Pay Attention*, and *Excellence in Education: The Oxford Learning Difference* and has served as president/CEO of Oxford Learning Centres, Inc. since 1984.

Oxford Learning Centre

Canadian Office
747 Hyde Park Road, Suite 230
London, ON N6H 3S3

Phone: 519-473-1207
Email: info@oxfordlearning.com
Website: www.oxfordlearning.com

CHAPTER 13

Booster Juice

“We’re making the world a better place, one smoothie at a time!”

Having always been a healthy eater and coming from a sports background, it was only natural that I would gravitate to a health-oriented business. Based on the way I thought the health and wellness movement was growing in Canada, I saw an opportunity. While travelling on business in the U.S., my interest was sparked by the juice bars I sporadically encountered on my excursions. Everyone knows that fruits and vegetables are a key component in promoting and sustaining good health. After all, studies have proven that fruits and vegetables provide us with essential vitamins, minerals, fiber, valuable fatty acids, complex carbohydrates, protein, antioxidants and other important substances. They have been attributed to reducing the risk of cancer, heart disease, chronic diseases and other ailments, plus fruits and vegetables are low in fat and calories. They are delicious, filling, refreshing, and can even satisfy a sweet tooth, while increasing your energy, strengthening your immune system, building stronger bones, and enabling your complexion to glow. Yet, while all this information is well known, ask most people and they will confess that they need to add more fruits and vegetables to their diet. I wanted to find an easy and efficient way to help people help themselves, and I knew Booster Juice was the answer.

Though I can't take credit for inventing the juice bar concept, I can take credit for having the vision to recognize that with some tweaks and modifications, juice bars would work in Canada too. Even though my family, friends, and mentors all thought I was crazy, I knew it was something I had to do. But there was a slight problem. I noticed that in the U.S. juice bars were usually found in the warmer weather regions. Whether it was California or Texas, the weather was a huge asset in selling their product, since it was incredibly conducive to quenching people's thirsty needs for refreshment. It was obvious that I wouldn't be able to use the same sales pitch here in Canada since people don't seek out refreshing cold drinks in sub-zero weather. Knowing that Canadians are value driven, I would need to focus on educating and promoting the enormous health benefits gained from consuming our products. Even though my support group simply could not envision people paying $4.00 for a cold, refreshing product in winter, I still followed my vision. So I walked away from a longstanding, very well-paying position as a mechanical engineer and decided to prove them all wrong. My gut feeling kept insisting that there was a growing awareness and interest in health and wellness in Canada, and that we were just at the tip of the iceberg.

Today Booster Juice has evolved into a truly unique food service concept that combines great tasting products with unparalleled convenience while promoting a "health, freshness, wellness" message in a fun, vibrant, colourful, and magnetic store environment. I've always believed that franchising was intriguing, and it was the best way to grow a brand fast. From the very beginning I knew in my heart that the concept was going to do very well as a franchise system, though I did have one fear. My fear was that someone with deep pockets would recognize what a great winner of a concept we had and would decide to open five or 10 juice bars all at once and pull the rug from under me. I knew I didn't have the money to saturate the market with Booster Juice locations as quickly as I would have liked to, and I also knew that organic growth would take too long to create massive brand awareness.

However, I was only worried long enough to realize that we only had ourselves to compete against. Even if there were hundreds of other juice bars, all we had to focus on was the quality of our business. The goal has always been to reach excellence in our category: our name, our brand and our service. Franchising provided us with the opportunity to get a huge running start into getting brand recognition and establishing ourselves in the Canadian market. In the first year we opened 15 stores, in the second another 35. Booster Juice rose from inception to 50 stores in two years. I was fortunate that I didn't make too many mistakes along the way, since growing too fast can be detrimental to a business's existence, especially if you don't have a strategic plan and a back-up plan in place.

I was married with a family when I started Booster Juice, and it was difficult in a number of ways. First of all, success requires a lot of hands-on attention, and being a perfectionist, I've always recognized that the company would need my full attention in order meet or exceed my expectations. I can tell you that no one will ever take care of your baby as well as you do. They don't have your vision, and they won't have the same burning drive or the emotional connection that you have. Therefore, even though I had staff and other support systems in the wings, I always wanted to make sure I knew where I wanted the brand to go, what the brand identity was, and I refused to just hand it over to someone else to take care of. On the other hand, I had to learn the art of balance within a much bigger infrastructure and how to still be involved in every single aspect of the business.

Talking to my friends, I realized that we were all walking on the tightrope of balance. Yes, there are stretches of time that you need to be more involved with one aspect of your life than another, but when that is done you balance it out by giving a little more to the area that was being neglected. To most people success is equated with a person's financial achievements; of course financial freedom is great but it is only one part of the puzzle we call life. My definition of success is determined by a person's overall balance in life, which includes the financial rewards that are reaped along the way for a life well spent.

Personally, I would advise future franchisors to be brutally honest and ask themselves a few simple questions since they are the ones that know themselves the best. First and foremost, do you have a positive outlook and do you enjoy being around people – all the time? These questions should be your deal breaker if the answer is no. If it is, you'd be smart to walk away. If you do not have good people skills or you don't enjoy people, then this is not a career choice for you. In the franchise world you will need to work with many different types of personalities, on many different levels and in many different capacities. Just as in any relationship, sometimes the experience will be great and sometimes not.

The next question would be, is your product a "franchisable" product? You will need to have a solid strategic plan ready and the list goes on from there. Aside from all the preparation and fortitude it takes to put together the business, you will also have to ensure that your franchises have all the tools necessary to be successful. The whole concept of franchising is that the franchisor has the responsibility to put together a well-functioning business model and everything necessary to create brand awareness with strong advertising and good marketing. Operational support is a must, because I find that there are times when people don't do the right thing, even when they want to. Having a strong operational team that can go out and coach the franchise partner is critical to assuring brand consistency and their future success.

I have to say I've been very fortunate that I have not made too many mistakes right from the start, because many times those mistakes can make or break your business. Since opening my business on November 13, 1999, I have never grown my business just for the sake of growing. I was more concerned with ensuring that the site choice would work and I always made sure that the rent I was paying was a good fit for my business model and my numbers. A lot of franchise locations have issues with shutting their doors even though they had a good jumpstart. We always hear about other concepts that had to shut down due to a variety of reasons; i.e., a great product that went under because the staff wasn't right, or because they couldn't meet a rent increase. However, it's rare to hear about the strategic reasons that were being played behind the scenes, like a location that grew amidst a changing neighbourhood and the business didn't move out of the area when their clientele left. There are so many different aspects to being a franchisor. You have to be an observant and intuitive multi-tasker that leads others to victory. It's not all about finding a product and letting people duplicate your business while you pocket the money. Bottom line is, it needs to be perfected, tweaked to grow with public demand, and it must be handled by you.

At this stage, Booster Juice really has very good brand awareness and coverage from coast to coast. I have an excellent advantage based on the fact that Canadians have very much embraced Booster Juice as their own. I have three times the number of stores as the next biggest competitor and more stores than all of the competition combined. From a branding perspective, we will continue to partner up with celebrities and athletes like José Bautista and other impressive sports figures like him. My goal is to continue to find innovative ways to keep flourishing. I want to ensure that the franchise partners are successful and excited about our product and that we are all making a difference while having fun along the way. I get the biggest thrill when franchises express their exhilaration about their financial stability and the contentment with their lives both professionally and personally. To me the true test of success is when an existing franchise partner purchases and opens more stores.

My commitment to my franchises and to life is that I will live by the "can do" attitude my grandmother instilled in me. It's about driving with my eyes looking out through the windshield and not steering with my eyes glued to the rearview mirror.
I can only wish the same for you!

Dale Wishewan

Co-Founder,
President and CEO

Booster Juice president and CEO Dale Wishewan has always been a team player. Born in Waskatenau, Alberta, Wishewan was involved in sports from a young age. He cultivated his love of baseball on the diamond near his home and hoped one day to get a shot at the big leagues.

Wishewan developed a competitive drive that fueled him to some of the highest national levels of baseball and curling. But his passion was balanced with a solid foundation of strong values, firm ethics and a positive attitude, traits that Wishewan credits his late grandparents for instilling in him.

In 1989, a baseball scholarship brought Wishewan to the state of Oregon where he was on his way to live his dream of playing major league baseball. Wishewan studied in the demanding faculty of mechanical engineering and tried hard to balance his studies with the schedule of a Division 1 baseball program. Injuries and a realization that getting drafted was becoming a long shot caused Wishewan to focus on completing his degree. Wishewan earned his Bachelor of Science from Portland State University in Mechanical Engineering.

Upon graduating, Wishewan joined a small, privately-owned company where he worked in international technical sales of pressure vessel components. But in 1999, Wishewan decided to pursue the start of his own company. He combined his love of staying active and living a healthy lifestyle into the juice and smoothie industry. Because such was practically non-existent in Canada at the time, Wishewan realized he had uncovered an untapped and potentially lucrative market.

Wishewan dedicated himself totally to researching and developing every component of the concept. Once he decided to feature nutritious, natural herbal supplements in each smoothie, Booster Juice was officially born.

Unlike many company founders, Wishewan always had a “product first” mentality. Rather than cut costs and focus on margins at the beginning, he was willing to pay the price for quality products, knowing that as the number of stores grew, he’d be able to negotiate better prices. Wishewan’s vision of and commitment to product excellence and value laid a solid foundation for the success of the company.

Booster Juice was up and running in a matter of months. The first store opened in Sherwood Park, Alberta, in November 1999. Since that time, over 300 Booster Juice locations have opened in Canada, the U.S., Saudi Arabia, the United Arab Emirates, the Netherlands, India, Mexico, and Brazil. Wishewan has received numerous accolades for his work with and vision for the company. In 2005 he received the Ernst and Young Entrepreneur of the Year award. In 2003, he was named one of Canada’s prestigious Top 40 Under 40 for his work in five key criteria areas including: vision and leadership; innovation and achievement; impact; community involvement and contribution; and strategy for growth. Wishewan also earned the 2004 Foodservice and Hospitality Entrepreneur of the Year award, and Booster Juice was recognized as one of Edmonton’s Top Twelve businesses in 2003.

Booster Juice is currently one of Canada’s top 50 restaurants with sales of approximately 110 million, and it continues to be one of Canada's fastest growing foodservice chains.

Although Wishewan never made it to the majors in baseball, his work with Booster Juice has brought him into the business big leagues. His successful guidance of the young company is an unquestionable entrepreneurial grand slam.

Booster Juice - Canada

#205, 8915 – 51st Avenue
Edmonton, Alberta
Canada T6E 5J3

Phone: 780-440-6770
Toll-Free: 1-800-505-5971
Email: franchise@boosterjuice.com
Website: www.boosterjuice.com

CHAPTER 14

Massage Addict

"A unique Canadian health care success story!"

Even though massage therapy has been used in different parts of the world throughout history, it wasn't long ago that medical professionals mocked the idea of massage as a practical therapeutic alternative. With the rise of the pharmaceutical industry and technical medical discoveries around the early 20th century, massage was never considered a serious contender in the therapeutic arena. If you asked any massage therapist 60 years ago about the future of massage, they could never have predicted the extent to which massage would grow. In the past 20 years, the massage therapy industry has been increasing in popularity in leaps and bounds, both as a personal service and as a valuable healthcare modality. Due to the commitment of some professional therapists and industry leaders, massage is amassing more recognition and respect than ever before. Undoubtedly the future of massage therapy, though not yet firmly defined, is full of excitement and possibilities. After all, the evolution of healthcare discipline is directly related to the ability to demonstrate therapeutic outcomes. Massage has been doing just that all along!

Groundbreaking studies on alternative medicine have shown a consistent pattern in this emerging field – that massage is becoming more established, increasingly in demand, a developing trend, and that the Canadian population is showing huge acceptance of this viable and valuable healing practice. My goal was to make massage therapy a luxury that everyone could afford. I was determined to turn Massage Addict into a national brand, and the fastest way I knew how to grow the brand was through franchising.

My name is Lori MacKenzie and at 29, after a back injury, I sought weekly massage therapy treatments. Coming from a franchise fitness membership background, I remember lying on the table and thinking to myself, "What if the therapist knew I was going to come back weekly? Would she charge me less?" And, "what if I was to commit to purchasing a bundle of massages at a time? Would that make a difference in the fee?" Playing around with this notion in my head for a while, I came up with the idea for a membership-based massage therapy service. That's what ultimately led me to what is now Massage Addict. Once my intuition identified the gap in the massage market for this particular service, I proceeded to get to work.

The first thing I did was put in some due diligence to make sure there was sufficient demand for the service. Then I developed a reasonable business plan, secured financing, and developed advertising, a website and content, etc. In 2009, only six months after deciding to go for it and just after our well-known international fitness franchises sold, my vision became my reality. Massage Addict became the first membership-based massage therapy service in Canada. You can imagine my surprise though, when within only three months of opening my first clinic, someone came in to inquire about opening a franchise location in Halifax.

Enter Chris Harker! Chris Harker, who had owned and operated a successful transportation business for six years, recognized the vision right away and became franchisee number one. This was the beginning of what was to become a great partnership between Chris and me. While Chris began running his clinic in 2009 in Halifax, Nova Scotia, I continued to work at selling, opening and supporting new franchises. Chris and I worked well together promoting and growing the brand of the first two operating clinics in Halifax. A year after opening the first clinic, I had six Massage Addict locations up and running.

Chris and I realized that we shared the same vision for the company, and our strengths complemented each other's. As a rule neither of us would recommend partnerships to others, but we were fortunate enough to have had the opportunity to work together before partnering up. It happened quite organically for us. Before long, it became quite evident that we could grow the company more effectively together. Chris and I officially became partners of Massage Addict Inc. in 2011.

Both Chris and I believe that our partnership is unique. We come up with our best plans and ideas when we collaborate and brainstorm together. We have the comfort and freedom to be open and air ideas with each other that may be out of the box, with no fear of judgment. It's amazing what great ideas can come from this freedom.

We don't have rules of who does what, but we definitely know each other's strengths. Brand and advertising is my forté and finance and sales are Chris's expertise. We have plans for continuing to develop the brand and add more locations in Ontario and on the west coast of Canada, reaching the 50 franchise mark. As to our future franchises, we look for self-motivated people who are eager to bring the Massage Addict brand to their community. It is also important to us that they are a bit like-minded and aligned with our business philosophy. Through our life experiences, Chris and I believe that the key to success is to surround ourselves with good people and great franchises, encouraging and fostering an environment that promotes everyone to share their ideas and experiences.

Both Chris and I also think that franchisees need to have a drive to succeed. While they do not need a degree, they do need to be within the spectrum of being an entrepreneur. There are people that will recognize a franchise brand and take the steps to become a franchisee and be satisfied with operating a successful business. Others will recognize a gap in the market for some product or service and take the steps to open a business that satisfies that demand in a profitable way. Both of these are entrepreneurs; they are just at different points of the spectrum. The bottom line is: loving what you do, being able to make money while doing it, and having the autonomy that comes with it. That is what we are all working towards.

Franchisor hopefuls need to do the legwork: find out what has worked for certain brands and gather as much information as possible prior to making a decision on what direction to take or how to grow. Furthermore, they will need to make sure to have a Disclosure Document and a good franchise lawyer and join organizations like the Canadian Franchise Association (CFA). There are many benefits to joining an association like the CFA for networking and sharing best practices from other franchise brands, learning from other franchisers' mistakes and maybe even establishing beneficial mentor relationships.

We did have our share of challenges but found those were the times when we gained many valuable lessons and insights into ourselves and each other. First and foremost, we have to acknowledge how lucky and fortunate we were to have partnered up with each other. Next, we recognize what an amazing support team we've had rooting for us along the way. This gave us the confidence, energy and fortitude to keep focused on what we had to do.

The media has and still does take quite an interest in Massage Addict. They helped us leave our thumbprint in Canadian history with interviews such as CBC radio, *Financial Post*, *Halifax Herald*, and many more. Our biggest breakthrough came in January 2012, when CBC's Dragons' Den TV Show showcased Massage Addict and its success on a national platform. The Dragons' ringing endorsements on the show resulted in an inundation of email leads from all over Canada just 10 minutes after the show aired (Season 6, Episode 13, last segment on the show). Of course, this, along with the support of our members, has been an incredible validation of our staff and services. This motivates us to continue growing so that we can help more people realize the benefits of therapeutic massage.

Let's face it: massage has been popularized by the rich and famous as the ultimate desirable pampering component. That's why when the average person thinks of a massage, very often visions of bliss and pampered delights float through that person's mind. We offer both relaxation and therapeutic massage. With massage therapy being covered by many people's extended health care plans, it is now easier than ever to experience the benefits of therapeutic massage by a Registered Massage Therapist. We have hundreds of appointments available every week, and we strive to book next day appointments when requested by our members.

New clients can feel free to tour our website, where they will find everything they need to know about our facilities, the services we offer, the health benefits that massage therapy provides and the benefits of becoming a Massage Addict member. It describes the types of massages we offer, which physical symptoms get maximum benefit from which therapeutic technique, and what to expect on their first visit. Appointments can always be booked online, and a personal Registered Massage Therapist will assess and plan a safe and specific treatment for their needs.

Massage Addict is here to serve people across Canada. Whether it is through our monthly membership massage program or by helping like-minded individuals to establish a fulfilling and profitable life as a franchisee, it is our goal to create a nation of Massage Addicts!

Lori MacKenzie

President and Founder

Lori Mackenzie was born and raised in Ontario and spent most of her youth in Niagara Falls. After high school she attended a three year business program in Barrie, Ontario.

She moved to Halifax and opened her first Curves franchise in October of 2001. It was a great success. In 2002, her and her husband opened their second location, and by January 2005, she was overseeing operations of four locations, including two in Quebec City. In January 2008 they sold the last two locations they acquired, and she began focusing on her next venture.

In July 2008, she opened Massage Addict in Nova Scotia. It was the first membership-based Massage Therapy Clinic in Canada. Members pay just $59 a treatment because they commit to coming once a month for a minimum of one year. That same year Lori also decided to franchise the idea and, in November 2008 she signed up Chris Harker, her first franchisee, in Halifax, Nova Scotia.

Chris and Lori worked together to build their brand and ultimately became business partners a few years later as the franchise began to grow. Currently, they have seven locations and five under construction that are set to open this fall.

Chris Harker

CEO

Chris was born in Cape Breton, Nova Scotia and has lived in Ontario and Nova Scotia. For the past 20 years he has lived in the Halifax area and he studied business at St. Mary's University in Halifax.

He joined Massage Addict in October of 2008 as franchisee number one. He and Lori worked together to build their clinics and developed a great working relationship. He partnered with Lori a few years later and they took Massage Addict to a new level. They appeared together on an episode of the CBC's Dragons' Den in January of 2012, which put Massage Addict in a national spotlight. They are now the market leaders of membership-based massage therapy in Canada. They are a unique Canadian health care success story and they are looking forward to continuing their rapid growth.

Massage Addict
52 Kinross Court
Fall River, Nova Scotia
Canada, B2T 0E4

Phone: 855-501-5017
Email: info@massageaddict.ca
Website: www.massageaddict.ca

CHAPTER 15

White Spot Restaurants

"We operate our business with three values. Integrity. Involvement. Innovation."

White Spot Limited has been in existence since 1928, making it one of North America's most beloved restaurant chains. As a young man, our founder Nat had a great passion for food and a love of people.

Nat started out selling peanuts and popcorn on city streets and moved to hot dogs, fresh roasted peanuts and coffee at Athletic Park in Vancouver. He transformed his 1918 Model T truck into a travelling lunch counter and parked it at Lookout Point on SW Marine Drive, where families would purchase their food, get back in their cars, and continue on their weekend drive.

On one particularly hot day in 1924, one of his guests at Lookout Point shouted from his car, "Why don't you bring it to us?" This was all the inspiration Nat needed, and in June of 1928, he opened White Spot Barbeque. It was an eatery located in the Marpole neighbourhood at 67th and Granville Street, known to many as Granville House. Nat actually wanted to name it the Granville Barbecue, but decided on White Spot when a friend suggested that he name it after a restaurant in Los Angeles. He liked the suggestion because White Spot reminded him of spotlessness and cleanliness, which he knew was an integral part of a restaurant experience. Through innovativeness and creativity, our legendary restaurant chain was born.

An example of Nat's ingenuity was when lines of drivers would be parked nearby and they asked if Nat or his staff could deliver the food to their cars. Nat then hired servers who "hopped to it" to do so. Canada's first car hops were created. In 1937, the White Spot Restaurant and Drive-In replaced the original log cabin BBQ as White Spot #1. But creativity can only go so far; great guest service is needed too. If you were to scan through the White Spot archives, our history and writings would reveal that Nat had a deep understanding of the importance of the guest. To this day, we still focus on his vision of good quality, family meals and burgers, spotless cleanliness, great guest services and innovative changes to enhance their dining experience.

White Spot has only had three stints of ownership. The first was Nat Bailey, the founder; then it was owned by General Foods for about a decade until Shato Holdings acquired it in 1982. Initially all of the locations were corporately owned. We began franchising in 1992 with our first franchise in Vernon, British Columbia. Franchising really gave us a chance to expedite the growth of White Spot throughout British Columbia, getting the taste of White Spot to more British Columbians and, of course, we've been successfully franchising ever since.

White Spot's credo is "Make a Difference." It's clear White Spot has and does, for our legions of guests and employees, the communities in which we operate, and our franchise business partners.

White Spot has over 1,600 corporate employees and well over 4,000 when combined with our franchises. Despite our size and history, the company has tremendous energy and continuously looks for ways to enhance the experiences we offer our guests and our employees, as well as to enhance the value and stability of our franchises' investments. For example, White Spot was the first restaurant to offer its culinary employees, both corporate and franchise, the opportunity to complete their nationally recognized Red Seal chef certification in-house.

White Spot Restaurants serve breakfast, lunch, and dinner in a comfortable and welcoming environment. White Spot is known for having a passion for using only the freshest and finest quality ingredients. We operate our business with three values: Integrity; Involvement; Innovation. Integrity is critical to any business; we need to make sure that we make the right decisions for the right reasons. We encourage our people to get involved, for as a team we are stronger. Finally, innovation is about being creative and staying on top of the market trends at all times so that we can be relevant in the marketplace. We conduct ongoing consumer research. We also survey our entire staff, managers and our franchises. We do a lot of listening to our people, making sure that we have a good pulse of what's going on within the organization while maintaining an open line of communication.

Currently we have 40 full-service franchise locations and 25 corporate White Spot locations. The fact that the company owns as many corporate locations as we do is something that our franchises really appreciate about us. We are just as invested as they are in continually evolving our brand and our concept. We are obviously focused on sales success for all of our stakeholders, but equally important is the bottom line profit for our franchises. We take great pride in the fact that we've been around for a long time, but we also know that our past success doesn't guarantee our future success. Therefore, even though we have become market leaders in western Canada, we continue to find ways of keeping relevancy in our brand so people who have known us for a long period of time and have been faithful patrons of White Spot will eagerly continue to do so.

The franchise relationship is a "co-dependent" one in a healthy way, as the franchisor and the franchisee depend on each other's success. The franchisor creates the vision and strategy and must mentor, assist and provide the tools that the franchises need in order to succeed in their business. The support team at our Home Office is made up of strong people who work cohesively on business plans to ensure success for the organization. That in turn is what assures the franchisee's success, and it keeps the machine in motion. Therefore, it is imperative for a potential franchisee to assess why this would be important for them and to move forward with confidence and clarity. It's a big decision to make.

We put together programs and packages, and now we've got a very vibrant franchise program within White Spot. We soon realized that, because of our level of involvement, many of our franchises proceeded to take on multiple locations. So when I get that commonly asked question, "What makes a good franchisee?" I say, "One of the most important factors is finding somebody that has as much passion for your brand and really cares about it as much as you do!"

To become a franchisee with White Spot, you don't necessarily have to have restaurant experience, but you do need to have a real passion for people. This is something you can't fake. To be successful in our industry strong interpersonal skills are an absolute must. The guest doesn't care if it's a corporate or franchise location; they just want to have a great experience. We also think, that as people are going through the process to acquire a White Spot, they need to do proper due diligence on us. We check them out as well, as we want to make sure that we have the same values and organizational points of view. Life is in the details. From the outside looking in, people have a tendency to see our business as an easy one, but little do they know how complicated and detailed it really is. Therefore, it makes it easier when you have like-minded people with a common goal working together.

The scrutiny of a strong corporate culture is a huge contributor to our overall success. I think it's imperative that an organization has driving principles that can thrust it into becoming and sustaining a successful business. I also believe that flawless execution of our restaurants is an extremely essential component, as well as the type of leadership we offer within our restaurants, in the industry, and in our communities. I think our story is as much a people story as it is about White Spot, since there's always great satisfaction when you surround yourself with great people, and we've got wonderful people working for us. We have more than 4,000 employees and millions of guests that have an expectation of what we're about. We always want them to feel and to know that we appreciate them and the fact that they are all part of our success.

We have had a lot of monumental moments at White Spot. We saw an opportunity to be innovative, and we developed a unique and proven "fast casual" concept. Triple O's offers high quality, unique tasting food made fresh, just for you. The Triple O's concept is comprised mainly of licensed and franchised locations outside of North America and into Asia. We currently have locations in Hong Kong, Singapore and mainland China.

There are just so many memorable occasions through the years that picking one is almost as difficult as choosing a favourite child. They're all so different and just as exciting. Success in the hospitality business is tremendously rewarding, but all of us in the industry know it isn't easy. Success over eight decades is extraordinary. Named one of Canada's Top 50 Best Managed Companies, and having received many awards for franchise excellence, White Spot has managed to keep the essence of its legendary brand, its loyal following, and the support of its franchisees while making changes to stay relevant and to attract new guests and new markets.

My mother would always say, "Make sure you leave things better than you found them." My dad would always remind me, "There's no substitute for hard work." George Tidball, an early mentor, always talked about the importance of the guest and being guest-focused, and the importance of really creating a culture where the most important thing in your business is the guest. He would always remind me to try to find ways of doing things differently or looking at them from different perspectives. I think the three pieces of advice together are a great formula to live by. I think we owe it to our franchises, our employees, to our guests and to ourselves to do so. Giving your best at all times is all you or anyone can expect of you. Here at White Spot we do just that, and it has been a blessing for us all!

Warren Erhart

President and CEO

Warren Erhart, a graduate of Malaspina College and recipient of the Vancouver Island University's (VIU) Most Distinguished Alumni award in 2010, is the president and CEO of White Spot Hospitality. In 1990, after spending 14 years with the Keg Restaurant group, Warren joined White Spot as the Division General Manager. In 1994 he was promoted to president and CEO. At this time White Spot had 35 locations with sales of $71 million.

White Spot Hospitality is now in over a hundred locations with sales of over $200 million dollars and will serve over 16,000,000 guests this year.

A major factor in Warren's success has been his ability to build relationships with employees, guests, and business partners, as well as his passion for giving back to the community. White Spot received the Corporate Hero award this year from Variety International.

Warren is currently the past chairman of the Canadian Restaurant Foodservice Association. He has served on the board since 1993. He was inducted into the British Columbia Restaurant Hall of Fame in 2010.

White Spot celebrates its 85th anniversary in 2013, making it one of North America's most enduring and best loved restaurant chains. White Spot has been the recipient of many industry awards and most recently was recognized as one of Canada's Top 50 Best Managed Companies.

White Spot Restaurants

1126 SE Marine Drive
Vancouver, BC V5X 2V7

Phone: 607-321-6631
Fax: 604-321-0367
Email: franchise-info@whitespot.ca
Website: whitespot.ca

CHAPTER 16

Concierge Home Services

Total Household Management

> *There's always a solution!*

After finishing my degree at the University in Ottawa and spending a year teaching overseas, I returned to my hometown of Toronto, Canada, where I started a career in Human Resources in the emerging Internet sector. It was very fast-paced and I loved every minute of responding to the changing needs of our growing company. My job soon turned me into a frequent flier between Toronto, Ottawa, and Montreal. I dealt with management and executives who were usually women struggling to balance career and home. Over lunches and in airport waiting areas, I listened to stories about their cleaning service breaking something, neighbours not feeding the cat, or a babysitting crisis, all while they were away from home. Then it struck me! If three women in three different cities were experiencing the same challenges in finding reliable help for their home, then here was an opportunity to fill a niche.

My idea came at a time when I was doing some serious soul searching. My boss had transferred me to Ottawa. This was a good move for me personally, because I love the city and have family here. However, it meant a new boss, a new work environment, and all the fun was gone from my job. The company had been absorbed into a large corporation and my work seemed to be more about filling out forms than solving real issues and meeting business goals. I knew I could stay for the big salary and juicy pension, but I dreaded the thought of going to work every day. It wasn't what I wanted for my life, and it certainly wasn't the example I wanted to set for my small daughter. I viewed this as the perfect opportunity to pursue my dreams, fill a niche, and start my own company.

While researching the market I learned there were two main sectors in the home cleaning industry: private individuals and large team-based cleaning companies. Based on all the complaints I had heard, it seemed there were issues inherent in both. So I decided to establish a business model that would combine the best of both worlds. The core of the business was going to be an operating system that would not only have all the security and stability of a large company, but also the personal touch of a private provider. In 2001, Concierge Home Services was launched from a corner in my unfinished basement with my little girl playing in another corner. I spent hours modifying and improving systems and procedures. I pulled her in a wagon while delivering flyers and crept out of the house to go to network meetings before she woke in the morning. I changed hats and clothes several times a day as I juggled being boss, manager, salesperson, marketing maven, cleaner, pet sitter, and mother.

Within a couple of years, all systems were running smoothly and one of my staff members started helping me in the office part time. By the time my youngest was born in 2005, all procedures and policies were fully documented. My part-time office helper had evolved into a full time manager who effectively ran the business, including customer service, scheduling, hiring, and quoting. I really had nothing to do beyond answering questions and doing some administrative work. It would not have been difficult to just keep coasting along, but as an entrepreneur with a vision of building the company beyond my living room and even beyond the boundaries of Ottawa, I couldn't just coast. Recognizing that Concierge Home Services was a concept that worked and could easily be taught to others I knew I had something to offer the world. The next step was to franchise.

I chose franchising to expand Concierge Home Services because the franchise model fit so well with our brand and culture. We build relationships with homeowners based on excellent customer service and communication. Since consistent house cleaning is what homeowners and professionals require most, it became our basic service. We also provide services to meet their household management needs and evolve with them as their needs and requirements change over time. When our clients travel, they trust us to care for their homes, plants, and pets. We offer home checks and pet sitting. We'll arrange for carpet cleaning, window washing, duct cleaning, upholstery cleaning, drapery cleaning or whatever is required. In a world filled with choices, it is easier for our clients to call us than to search and select a provider to meet their household needs. People are increasingly looking for ways to un-complicate their lives. What is easier than having one company provide all of these services?

Success is never a straight line, and I've made plenty of mistakes along the way. When I started in franchising, it felt a little like wandering in the desert. I searched online and in books for information about franchising. I connected with the Entrepreneurship Centre in Ottawa. I cold-called emerging franchisors and I gathered everything I could find like a magpie. Yet so much of what I learned wasn't applicable to my business. Our concept didn't fit neatly into any one category; although we are home-based, we hire and manage staff, we offer more services than a residential cleaning company, but we aren't an errand running company. I believe that every mistake is a learning opportunity, and I strongly feel that the detours over the past few years have helped me understand how to be a better franchisor.

It took a year to prepare our franchise model, and just after joining the CFA (Canadian Franchise Association) we opened our first franchise in southern Ottawa. My family also moved into a new home, and the business moved into a new headquarters office in a professional building. Franchising to me was a partnership between the system and the franchises that operate it. I felt that having a franchise partner in each community would position us better in duplicating our system of building trusting relationships with our clients. Setting up a centralized call centre and hiring a team of managers is impersonal and didn't fit well with our brand of personal attention. Our clients prefer having a more approachable Concierge Home Services franchise in their area and would be more likely to trust them with arranging their personal services.

Clarity comes with experience, and after being in business 11 years, it gets easier to know how to identify what skills are required in order to be a successful franchisee, and what the client demographic is – our clients are busy homeowners and professionals aged 30-60. Baby Boomers are a huge growing sector. Our customers value our integrity, our attention to detail, our customization of services, and our personal customer service. They know they could find someone to do it cheaper, but they understand the importance of insurance and accountability. They love the ease of trusting one company to access their home and provide a complete spectrum of household management services.

Successful Concierge Home Services franchises are good communicators who are active in their business communities. Networking, meeting new people, and developing referral relationships is a big part of the job. Managing staff, scheduling services and customer service is another component. Experience in our industry isn't necessary. We look for people with strong customer service and organization skills. Our training covers every aspect of our systems, and the ongoing mentorship and support helps franchises through every stage of growing their business. I tell all interested and prospective franchises, "If you can roll with the punches, you'll have a lot of fun and a lot of variety, since every week is different. After all, how many people wake up in the morning and know they are going to help someone that same day?"

After almost five years of franchising, we are at an interesting and exciting stage of our business. Our franchise team has developed and expanded, and much work has been done to strengthen the framework that supports the growth of our franchise network. Our operating manual and reporting system is all cloud-based. Benchmarking and measurements of our key metrics (KPI's) have been established. Two years ago, I left the lonely sands of the desert and entered a busy, friendly oasis. Social media has enabled me to connect with people in franchising all over the world and to build relationships with other women in franchising. I've established a team of people who believe in the unique qualities of our concept and who are excited about working towards the expansion of our franchise network.

Recently, I was asked to speak at my alma mater, Carleton University. The topic was "How to Use your Degree in Business." The theme which emerged was to keep moving towards your goal, even if the results are not immediately clear. I can look to people I work with now and trace the connection through three other people, resulting from a cold call I made five years ago. Making that phone call to move towards my goal created a chain of connections and introductions, which is now visibly making a difference in the growth of my company. The message here is to keep focused on your vision; don't let what appears to be a setback deter you from your goal.

Like motherhood, franchising is not what I anticipated. It is more complex than I ever imagined, though very rewarding, and I couldn't love the challenge more. Our concept allows women to use their management skills to build a business from their home and still have the energy and time for their family and themselves. By following our system, they can ramp up growth, avoiding all the mistakes I made so many years ago from the basement of my home. At the home office, we often look back, never forgetting where we came from. We've seen it all and can advise our franchises on just about any situation they encounter. Anyone who wants to be the boss and run a business which has all the kinks worked out should consider franchising. Being a franchisee means being a business owner within a framework which is invested in your success.

Rebecca Page

Founder

What does it take to be a successful entrepreneur? Just ask Rebecca Page, who is a trailblazer, with a keen eye for recognizing good opportunities. In her story, you learn Rebecca's brilliance and insights on setting goals and articulating a vision. An inspiration to all business owners, whether they are just starting out, or whether their aspirations are to achieve even more success, Rebecca shows you how to recognize the need for change and finding solutions, and the importance of timing and implementation.

Growing up in Toronto, Rebecca Page showed early entrepreneurial flair. She organized and promoted a book sale on her front lawn. Once, she wrote a newsletter which she sold in the school yard for five cents a copy. After graduating from Carleton University in Ottawa and then working overseas, she landed back in Toronto as an Human Resource professional for an Internet company. Rebecca loved the dynamic, fast pace until her company moved into a large corporate structure. Losing the opportunity to create and to problem-solve prompted her to pursue her early dream to build her own business. By this point, she had returned to Ottawa to be closer to family, and knew that the capital was an ideal place to launch.

She was inspired to start Concierge Home Services after hearing so many stories from stressed out managers who struggled to find reliable help to outsource household chores. Rebecca's extensive research revealed a market demand for a full service household management solution. She spent a year developing the branding and the business model that would fill that niche.

In 2001, Rebecca left her corporate cubicle and started Concierge Home Services in a corner of her basement. Knowing that homeowners require more than regular home cleaning, she created a one-stop shop for all household management services such as window washing, home checks, and carpet cleaning. She built the business on the foundation of integrity, respect for staff, and work-life balance. These values are still an integral element of the Concierge Home Services brand. Her motivation to help others build a profitable business which offers home-life balance is what drives her franchising success.

Rebecca lives in Ottawa with her husband Roland, two daughters, and a step-daughter. She is an avid reader and values time with her family as much as she loves building her business. She enjoys contributing to her community, especially to causes which support women and families. She currently sits as Vice President of the Board for Harmony House Women's Shelter, and has mentored businesswomen at Ottawa's Entrepreneurship Centre.

Rebecca's recognition includes the 40 Under 40 Award from the Ottawa Business Journal. Concierge Home Services won the Torch Award for Marketplace Ethics from the Better Business Bureau twice, and received the Canadian Franchise Association Franchisee's Choice Designation in 2011 and 2012.

Check out Rebecca's blogs about entrepreneurship, franchising, and motherhood at: rebeccapage.ca.

Concierge Home Services

Franchise Head Office
1376 Bank Street, Suite 302
Ottawa, Ontario
Canada K1H 7Y3

Phone: 613-523-9441 Ext. 1
Email: franchise@conciergehomeservices.com
Website: www.conciergehomeservices.com

CHAPTER 17

the Lunch Lady

> ***"It's not what happens in life that matters, it's what happens next!"***

All concepts have their humble beginnings, including the Lunch Lady! Who knew that my chance idea would turn into a distinctly Canadian solution to the absence of cafeterias in elementary schools? The Lunch Lady is like a restaurant on wheels for kids at school and has built success by offering busy parents a healthy alternative to the task of packing school lunches at home. We offer updated versions of traditional lunchtime favourites, redesigned with kids' good health and the Canada Food Guide in mind. Our lunches arrive at the right time and at the right temperature to be enjoyed as soon as the lunch bell rings. No parent volunteers or school staff members are required to assist with any part of the process. The Lunch Lady really does it all!

The Lunch Lady provides each child with their own individually catered meal that is pre-ordered and pre-paid by the parent. Meals can be ordered by paper menu or online on our safe and secure order site. A complete meal averages $5 - $6.00, which includes applicable taxes and usually a contribution to the school. We also offer alternatives and menu modifications for children with allergies, medical conditions and food preferences so that our programs are open to everyone who wants to participate. Once an order has been placed, it can be changed or cancelled for a credit to use another time. Parents can even cancel an order for a sick child up to 8 a.m. on delivery day.

Our meals are prepared fresh daily in inspected, nut-free, individually owned commercial kitchen facilities operated by our dedicated franchises, who take pride in the meals they deliver to their schools. Each of our franchises works hard to fulfill the promise of our brand, which is to deliver peace of mind to busy parents and a well-managed and reliable service to the school. We take pride in our menus and our food, using high quality, name brand ingredients to create options we know kids will enjoy. Our franchises in turn are supported by a dedicated Head Office team that is committed to everyone's success.

I am so fortunate to be able to say that today, the business I founded in 1993 has evolved into a nationally recognized brand. The Lunch Lady is proud to have contributed to a healthier food environment for kids at school, created careers for the brand's own franchises and competitors alike, provided hundreds of jobs for moms who want to work while the kids are in school, raised hundreds of thousands of "Hassle-Free" fundraising dollars annually for schools, and funded nutrition programs for schools in need through our relationship with Breakfast for Learning.

So how did a middle-aged mom raised in Oshawa, Ontario, with a history degree and virtually no food service experience become the Lunch Lady? I get asked this all the time. It is a really good story, and I enjoy sharing it.

Necessity, as they say, is the mother of invention. Necessity was certainly knocking on my door in 1992. I was a 40 year (and a bit) mom with two little kiddies, one autistic, with a husband who, as a consulting engineer, was very worried about a downturn in the economy. What would we do if I needed to contribute to the family income or provide supplemental income to fund therapies for our boy? Who would hire me? I would always be taking time off for appointments with doctors and specialists. What could I do on my own that allowed me to set my own schedule?

I found a book at the library called *Patchwork Economics*, which talked about creating a basket of odd jobs which when pieced together made a real job. If one was not going well, you could make income from the other. I considered everything from doing taxes and making artificial flower arrangements to putting together scrapbooks for other people. One of the ideas was to buy sandwiches from a deli and sell them to workers in office buildings. This is the idea that ended up "morphing" into the Lunch Lady. The truth is, I could have easily picked one of the other ideas and become the Flower Lady or the Memory Lady and then this would be a whole different story.

My goal was to work in the morning, and spend afternoons at therapies and appointments. The idea of a LUNCH business fit perfectly into this schedule, but there was a hitch. In 1992, I really did not know how to cook!

After the early death of my mom, neither I nor my dad developed an aptitude in the kitchen. We ate out of cans instead. Dad, a General Motors employee and a United Church lay minister, gave me advice while the daily ration of tinned beef stew was heating on the stove. While I have long forgotten the taste of the stew, I have never forgotten what he said to me. One of things he said was, "almost any skill can be learned if you are willing to do the work."

The "not cooking" was seen more as an inconvenience than a deterrent to my success. In the '80s I had started a vertical blind manufacturing business in Montego Bay (yes, in Jamaica) without knowing how to make window blinds, and I had figured that out. Surely I could learn how to cook.

Once I had made peace with the food preparation aspect of the job, imagine my surprise when I learned that the market was not yet ready for school lunches. No parent or school wanted my services. It seemed like such a good idea to me that I just could not understand why everyone else did not think so too. I had been so sure of my idea that I had signed a three year lease for a commercial kitchen on Woodbine Avenue in Markham, Ontario.

Most school administrators considered my service to be totally frivolous. "Surely parents can manage to put together a sandwich!" I heard. After all, in 1993, the widely held belief was that only kids in economically depressed areas needed food programs. No one considered that nutrition could be adversely affected by the pressures of an emerging culture that left working parents struggling to make time for a home life. That would come later.

But the reality, even in 1993, was that there was a crisis brewing. The snack food industry was exploding, and kids from nice middle class neighbourhoods had lunch pails full of brand-name empty calories. A trend had started that would continue to worsen and cause increasing anxiety among parents, school administrators, and public health officials alike. Without knowing it, I had seen the future.

But in 1993, I was oblivious to what was coming and had to pay the rent until the future arrived. I went out in search of customers wherever I could find them. I made lunches for auto shops, doctor's offices, small business owners and seniors, but I was not making enough lunches to meet my expenses. Every month, after I had maxed out my credit cards (the start-up financing being long gone) I asked my spouse or my dad for money to shore up my money pit of a business. There were days when I cried my eyes out, listening to the Moody Blues on the tape deck while driving all over town to make my deliveries, worrying about the future and combating my own self doubt and despair. I'd dry my eyes just in time to put my "smile" face on, deliver the lunches, then immediately start tearing up the moment the door closed back behind me.

However, of course, as the future is bound to do, it did arrive! Today the "Catered School Lunch Program" is a vibrant and growing multi million dollar business that is springing up in communities all across Canada, and it all started with an idea. As with so many businesses, it was a solution to a need.

As my husband likes to say, I have become an overnight success after 20 years of hard work! It has certainly been a journey, but when I think about it, it has not been so much about what has happened along the way but more about what has happened next.

There are two Lunch Lady stories. The first is the story of my first Lunch Lady kitchen and its many ups and downs, which included the high of the first school and the low of a failed attempt at partnership in year two. But through it all, my goals for the business did not change that much. I wanted to keep busy, spend time with the children, make a little income and take my son to speech therapy. I had not really thought very far beyond that.

The decisions I made next changed my relationship with my business forever.

As my business started to experience serious growth, I had a decision to make. I could just feel the energy that was being attracted to the Lunch Lady brand, and it was too strong to resist. I just had to find a way to grow my concept in a way that fit in with my values and ideals. My dad always used to say, "money works best when everybody has some," so with that in mind, I thought that maybe there were others out there just like me who were looking for the same type of opportunity I had created for myself. I liked the idea of sharing my business concept with others, and although I did not know much about franchising, I was interested to learn more.

Franchising is all about joining with others to fast track the growth of your concept and your brand, but it is also about shifting the focus of your brand from yourself to the opportunity you are creating for others.

And there is so much to learn. Starting a franchise is like starting a brand new business. It is not at all like operating your own concept, and it is not for the faint of heart. All your decisions must now serve the common good of your brand and all its members who are earning their living by being a part of your big idea. Decisions are made that will not please everyone, even though they are made to serve the overall well-being of the organization. The franchisor sets the rules and the franchisee follows them. It is like a dance that works when everyone is dancing to the same tune and shares a mutual enjoyment of the music. But nothing is perfect. Someone is always falling out of step. When this happens, all the other dancers are waiting to see what will happen next. What they must see is consequences for non-compliance that are both fair and swift so that everyone else can get back to the dance.

I love dreaming up new ideas, but I am not good with the details required to turn these ideas into reality. It is a big joke in our organization that I can be easily distracted by anything shiny. That is why it is absolutely essential that you acknowledge your own limitations and surround yourself with the people who enjoy the aspects of your business that you have little or no aptitude for.

So, I may be the face of the Lunch Lady, but I am definitely not the creator of the Lunch Lady Group. That has been a team effort. The Lunch Lady brand may be an expression of my personality, but the franchise system that supports it is a testament to the skills, passion, dedication and experience of my partners and my head office team and franchises, whose knowledge, energy and ideas have enriched our organization.

The franchise journey began in 1999 when I went looking for someone to assist me with the transition and found chartered accountant Jim Essex. Together, with our growing team, we have built a strong head office, created a brand serving over 1,100 schools in four provinces via a network of nearly 50 franchisee-owned and operated commissary kitchens. We have participated in healthy schools legislation, advocated for healthier food environments in Canadian schools and pestered big food companies to bring healthier fare to Canadian tables. We strongly support the Canadian Franchise Association, and have had the benefit of wonderful mentors like Mac Voisin, founder of M&M Meat Shops, and Stan Newman, former president of Colour Your World, who joined the company to assist with our corporate plan.

Despite failed partnerships in the past, the collaborative model still works best for me. I enjoy the support of my partners and the wisdom of their experience and expertise. I enjoy being part of a team. Partnerships work best when everyone's roles are clearly defined and the parties place a high value on mutual respect. This can save the day during times of disagreement.

Although we are equal partners, I work full-time, Jim part-time and Stan on an advisory basis only. This works for us. While I do have the most say on a day to day basis, I must also respect the abilities of those who have been hired to fill specific roles and give them the opportunity to make their own contribution. I don't want to be known as the franchisor who didn't know when to stop talking and start listening!

I think the decision to franchise my concept has also been to create the large extended family I did not have as a child. That family gets even bigger when I have the opportunity to spend time with my peers in the franchise industry, many of whom you will learn about in the pages of this book. They all have amazing stories of perseverance, struggle and true grit. I am totally in awe of their successes. I love being part of that energy and that journey.

The franchise industry is the backbone of the Canadian economy, and it is totally awesome to be a part of it. When I see the successes enjoyed by our own franchises, I feel immense satisfaction and pride, sensing that somehow all my efforts (and frustrations) have been for a purpose.

My dad used to say that we are all pebbles in each other's ponds and that each of us has a meaningful role to play while we are on this earth. I was hugely influenced by the pebbles my father dropped in my pond. Some have rippled on to affect others and perhaps you too as I share his wisdom with you:

- Be thoughtful. It is the little kindnesses that count
- Measure your words. Once they are out of your mouth they are public property
- Profanity is for people with limited vocabularies
- Value, but do not live in fear of, the opinions of others
- Take responsibility for your successes and your failures
- Remember to say thank you
- Make time for quiet reflection
- Some people will not like you and life is not always fair. Accept these realities with grace
- Almost any skill can be learned if you are willing to do the work
- We are ALL our brother's keeper. Make a difference in the lives of others
- Money works best when everybody has some

Today, I can honestly say that I am a good cook! I am also an energetic advocate for healthier school food for kids, the proud winner of numerous business awards, an active supporter of the Canadian Franchise Association, a dedicated volunteer, an appreciative partner, the proud employer of a wonderful team, a speaker, the subject and author of various articles, a TV guest, a sympathetic ear for busy parents and an optimistic mom and wife who perseveres daily to create the life she wants for herself, her family, and the other members of her growing brand.

And I cannot wait to see what happens NEXT!

Ruthie Burd

Founder

Ruthie Burd was raised in Oshawa, Ontario, the adopted and only child of James and Jean Young. After the early death of her mother, she was raised by her father, a self-educated lay preacher, who had a profound influence on her future beliefs and attitudes. Educated at McMaster University, Ruthie has enjoyed a varied and interesting career since graduating top of her class with a degree in History.

She had done everything from teaching work skills to special needs adults in a sheltered workshop in Hamilton and tax courses for H&R Block, to founding and operating a window blind manufacturing company in Montego Bay, Jamaica in the '80s.

In 1993, her need to create a business that worked around her autistic son's therapy sessions resulted in the creation of the Lunch Lady, a going concern that is still her full time vocation. She has become passionate about building her brand while contributing to the success of others, promoting a healthier attitude to food, encouraging parents to take back control of their cupboards, and persuading food companies to produce healthier options for the Canadian public.

Like all entrepreneurs, she has had her shares of ups and downs, but being a determined optimist, she has always found the necessary reserves she needs to forge ahead from within herself or those around her. Some days, the responsibility of being the person in charge can be pretty wearing, but never so overwhelming that she would want to do anything else.

Although the Lunch Lady began as a lunch service provider for elementary school children, many other food service opportunities are presenting themselves. The company is now in a period of transition, evolving from a school year-based business to a year round operation serving an expanded client base. Ever curious, Ruthie is looking forward to seeing what will happen next for the Lunch Lady brand.

When she is not the Lunch Lady, Ruthie is the proud mom of three boys, Chris, Brendan and Dylan, one daughter-in-law, Kara, and a cat named Catty-Cat. She is also married to the world's greatest husband, David, who has been her rock through thick and thin. Like most other busy working moms, she goes home to the laundry and has more tasks on her To Do list, than time to do them. Although she had a slow start in the kitchen (she and her dad embracing the convenience of tinned beef stew on a nightly basis after the death of her mother), today she is an accomplished and creative cook embracing a gluten- and dairy-free diet at home.

A self proclaimed and unapologetic workaholic, Ruthie appreciates it when David reminds her that everyone now and then needs some "down time." She loves to read, dance and daydream, eat chocolate, spend time with her husband and family, see friends and experience those rare and refined moments when she feels totally at peace with the world and everything around her feels just like velvet.

You can learn more about Ruthie and the Lunch Lady business she created at www.thelunchlady.ca.

the Lunch Lady

Head Office
151 Spinnaker, Unit #11
Concord, Ontario
Canada L4K 4C3

Phone: 905-660-5994
Toll-Free: 1-800-603-6656
Email: franchise@thelunchlady.ca
Website: www.thelunchlady.ca

CHAPTER 18

Union Burger

ub

union burger
FRESH BURGERS AND HAND CUT FRIES

"Quality is just the beginning..."

Looking back in time, history books validate that ground beef has been shaped into patties and eaten all over the world throughout the centuries. Not only is hamburger the most eaten food in the world, it is said that in North America, you can map out a trip from coast to coast by connecting hamburger joints, like an astronomer connects stars.

The history of ground meat has truly been through a meat grinder itself. One interesting anecdote states that the hamburger was most likely named after a popular steak in Hamburg, Germany, just as a few other meat products suggest a

German-Austrian connection as well, e.g., "frankfurters" from Frankfurt, Germany and "wieners" from Wien (Vienna), Austria. But there is a dispute as to who should get the credit for inventing the first hamburger sandwich. You can actually take your pick, since there are many in the running for the title, all of which claim to be the first to put hamburgers on bread. We may never know who really came up with the hamburger on a bun concept, but we do know that hamburger joints are one true North American culinary invention that now spans over 100 countries on six continents. Although we at Union Burger can never claim to be the originators of the hamburger or the burger sandwich, we strive to be the best at serving them!

At Union Burger we are redefining food that is fast by providing the highest quality product distinctively, as you like it, and all at a competitive price. Generally speaking, the thin hamburger patties, as well as many of the other food products served at fast food establishments, are mass-produced in factories and are frozen while in transit to their location. Hamburgers have come a long way since being served with ketchup, mustard, onions and pickles on a bun. All over the world people are finding new innovative angles and variations on serving up the classic burger, but what are they doing about the quality of the beef they are serving? It is unfortunate that because of the quality of beef they serve, fast food establishments and especially hamburger joints have developed a bad rap and a low class reputation. At Union Burger we are just as concerned about the high quality nutrition that we serve as we are about the taste of the food. Our fresh burgers, hand-cut fries and other menu items do not have to be doused with ketchup, mustard, onion and pickles in order for them to be palatable, though we do have a few innovative variations of these all our own to exhilarate our customers.

When my brother and I sold our sub shop and decided to pursue our individual dreams, I knew it was my time to begin my life mission that I always talked about. I could now begin to help others, but I had to make it first. I knew that by creating comfortable and hospitable family eateries that provided the best quality of food possible, I would be able to help not only the people I employed, but the customers too. My first franchise, Crabby Joe's Tap & Grill, evolved from the experience I gained and from the love I developed for the hospitality business. Franchising was the best way I knew how to help others succeed in life in a big way. The second franchise, Coffee Culture Café & Eatery, was developed from the need I saw in the marketplace for a place that is not a bar, but where people can congregate for periods of time and enjoy social interactions with friends, family, colleagues or whomever. This concept too was created with helping people in mind.

Union Burger, my third franchise, evolved from a necessity that I saw for better nutrition in the fast food industry. It was quite obvious that there was a need for a major overhaul in the fast food industry, and I knew what I could do to help. As people started being more aware of what they ate, their taste preferences were leaning more towards fresh products, though they still wanted to enjoy their comfort food. Here again, I wanted to help others to help themselves, whether they were consuming the food or serving it. So with the help of some colleagues, a marketing firm, and my own ingenuity we came up with the Union Burger name and concept. The idea was to bring together the perfect "union" of all the freshest ingredients available and to create a safe and healthy comfort food zone.

Our 100% premium beef hamburgers are always fresh, cooked to order, and contain no fillers or artificial preservatives. But the quality doesn't stop there. Union Burger also offers quarter pound all beef Angus Hot Dogs and All Natural Chicken. For the carb-conscious people out there, all of our burgers and chicken sandwiches are available in a wrap as well. Our fries are always hand-cut fresh every day and cooked in high quality, trans-fat free canola oil. For beverages, aside from the regular variety soft drinks, we serve good old fashioned milk shakes, handmade using real ice cream and milk. And although it's a bit unusual for a fast food establishment, Union Burger also serves up a nice chilled beer. Union Burger offers a wide variety of menu choices from your regular burger or cheeseburger topped the way you like it to a number of signature burgers we have created, such as our widely popular Bourbon Burger, or our Great Canadian Burger. The casual, upbeat metro décor along with the rock and roll music in the background are an added promise to enhance the diner's experience even more. Even though Union Burger is so completely different than our other establishments, I can assure you that they are all based on the same concept; great quality food, great fun and great service!

Franchising to me is the gift that keeps giving. First and foremost, franchising provides you as an individual a huge opportunity to change your life and to impact the lives of others on so many different levels. As you grow, franchising gives you the opportunity to impact your community, your city, your province, your country, your world

– and someday maybe even the entire world. It gives you a lot of possibilities and allows you to pace how big or how small, how fast or how slow you want to grow. Once you have a well-functioning system that you believe in, you can then clone it and keep sharing more of it with the world. It is important to love what you do, to come from integrity in every situation, to go the extra mile whenever possible, to love being around people and to want to help them, and to always function with a positive state of mind and with good intentions.

Once you realize that each location represents the brand that represents your name, you will begin to see that each successful franchise is a vote of reassurance that your concept is making a difference in people's lives. Although it may take some time to create a huge change of consciousness, every change begins with a single step. Our franchises are all geared to provide only the best quality of food, great ambiance, comfortable seating and efficient service. Everyone knows there is strength in numbers, so the more successful we become, the more franchises we will have. The more franchises we have, the more others take notice. The more others take notice, the more they may become more health conscious in their menu choices too. We the franchisors are the pioneers – the visionaries who see how we can make the world a better place with the idea we bring to the marketplace. We the people have the power to change the world by choosing where we spend our money. That is why it is important to surround yourself with like-minded people, whether they are partners or employees, who share your business vision and believe in your brand and are motivated to grow their business.

I believe there are three final components that at times get overlooked. To me these are vital to any aspect of success in business or in your daily life. Number one is to listen to your intuition. Without it, I could have missed out or delayed some monumental times for our business, like when we moved our headquarters from London, Ontario to Toronto, Ontario. Relocating to a bigger and more metropolitan market, at that particular time, availed us opportunities that we could not have foreseen. The second life tool that I would consider to be imperative is having good common sense, like having the common sense to seek out professional staff and take care of the core staff in our company to help our brands and franchisees grow. Lastly, one must find balance. I think Confucius said it best when he said, "Man is happiest while pushing a boulder up a mountain, but once he's on top he must find the perfect balance to stay there!"

Gus Karamountzos
Founder

Gus Karamountzos was born in Karya, Greece on October 2, 1960. He was the youngest of three children, the oldest a sister and the middle child a brother. He was raised in a small village in extreme poverty. Gus' father was a farmer, and his mother helped out where she could along with all of her household chores. When Gus was 10, the family moved to a bigger town with a population of 35,000. There the family was able to start a new way of life and were fortunate to take advantage of the education that was available to them at the time.

In 1977 at 17 years old, Gus was encouraged by his parents, but especially his father, to join his brother in Canada in an attempt to make an even better life for himself. His father knew that there would be more opportunities in Canada and he wanted the brothers to reunite. Although he left behind a lot of family members, including his father, mother and sister, Gus ventured into the world to create a new and better life for himself.

Gus immigrated to Stratford, Ontario where he joined his older brother, along with a

few distant relatives who had left Greece before he did. He worked in restaurants in odd jobs in the kitchen and as a cook. He met Helen, a beautiful Greek woman, whom he married in 1982 in Toronto, where she lived and had just graduated from Ryerson University. In 1983, they celebrated the birth of their first son, Peter. In 1984, a second son George was born and in 1988 his daughter, Tina, joined the family too.

While raising his family, Gus put all his efforts into working and building equity so that he would be able to survive and raise a family. Helen mostly stayed home raising the children along with help from the children's grandparents, and she helped Gus as much as possible in the family-operated restaurant. Gus continued to open individually operated restaurants. With his experience, his passion for food and cooking, and his experience operating the kitchens, he was able to operate each of the restaurants and made enough to provide for his family. It was his passion for the restaurant business, his commitment, drive and perfectionism that led Gus into many business opportunities, including Crabby Joe's Tap & Grill, Coffee Culture Café & Eatery, and Union Burger.

As the years went by, after many sacrifices and relocations, Gus and his family made the Greater Toronto Area their home and business headquarters, which today manages and operates more than 250 properties and restaurant locations throughout Canada and the United States.

Union Burger

2556 Meadowpine Blvd.
Mississauga, ON L5N 6P9

Phone: 905-813-8030
Email: info@ubburger.com
Website: http://www.ubburger.com/

Afterword

> ***"There is one quality which one must possess to win, and that is definiteness of purpose, the knowledge of what one wants, and a burning desire to possess it.***
> ***— Napoleon Hill"***

Whether you are yearning to become an entrepreneur or need to hone the entrepreneurial skills you already have, your decision to read ***Great Canadian Franchise Stories*** was a great first step. After all, this book was written with you in mind. We all know that best practices are the key to positive outcomes, so we compiled this book full of motivating and inspirational stories from proven successes to give you the confidence to pursue your dreams. Within these pages you have found an amalgamation of all the key elements you need to fulfill your greatest potential.

Learning is a constant process for everyone. History shows that having an experienced and successful mentor is one of the most effective ways to achieve positive results. Bill Gates learned from Warren Buffett. Larry Page turned to Michael Bloomberg and Steve Jobs. Canada's 2012 Chief Financial Officer of the year, Colleen Johnston of Toronto Dominion Bank Group, was tutored by the steady hand of Ed Clark. Whether you want to build a legendary blue chip company or start a successful franchise, you can never underestimate the importance of a great mentor. ***Great Canadian Franchise Stories*** gathers the wisdom, knowledge, and experiences of some of the greatest Canadian franchise mentors, who have generously shared their stories of how they overcame all obstacles in their determination to create their own success.

There is no substitute for experience, and in ***Great Canadian Franchise Stories*** you have accessed the accumulated experiences of these great franchise pioneers. Just by reading ***Great Canadian Franchise Stories*** you have gained a wealth of information to inspire and lead you to achieve whatever you believe. You have found all the data you need to develop a new sense of awareness. As you take time to really absorb all this advice and information, you will find yourself enveloped by a sense of security, assurance, and confidence when making professional and personal decisions on your road to a more balanced and successful life. Now that you have seen the world through the eyes of these amazing giants, you can learn from their trials and tribulations and know how to:

- Find and follow your passion.
- Focus on what you need to go to the next stage.
- Map out the landscape ahead.
- Transition more easily onto your destined path.
- Detect and correct problems early on.
- And so much more!

This book has provided you with an unparalleled opportunity to be mentored by these exceptional men and women who have shared their experiences of how and why they pursued their passion and climbed their way to the top.

In writing this book, I hope I have encouraged you to dream the impossible dream and step into your power now! I want you to believe in yourself enough to take the leap of faith that will propel you to create the life you want. I would love to see you become one of the next ***Great Canadian Franchises Stories***. I would be elated to have you join us at the top. After all, no one deserves it more than you!

Editorial Gems

Osler, Hoskin & Harcourt LLP
Franchise Law Group

Why Choosing the Right Law Firm is Critical to Your Success in Franchising

Introduction to the Franchise Legal Landscape

This timely book tells a number of stories of successful Canadian franchisors in diverse industry segments. Their success is a tribute to the vision, entrepreneurialism and diligence of their founders and, no doubt, the commitment and spirit of their franchises. However, in view of the complexity of franchise and other laws which impact the establishment, growth and operation of franchise systems, almost certainly these and many other successful franchisors have relied on experienced franchise law firms to manoeuvre through the legal and business aspects of franchising by providing proactive, creative and practical advice incorporating best practices in the industry.

There are currently five provinces in Canada that have enacted franchise legislation. They are, in chronological order, Alberta, Ontario, Prince Edward Island, New Brunswick and Manitoba. In addition, franchise agreements in Quebec are interpreted under the general contract rules of that province's Civil Code.

All Canadian franchise legislation is founded on two major principles. The first is that the franchisor must provide a prospective franchisee with a disclosure document which outlines in considerable detail, in response to specific prescribed items, the franchise being offered so the franchisee can make an informed investment decision. The document must be provided at least 14 days before any payment or agreement is signed relating to the franchise. Failure to comply with this disclosure requirement grants a franchisee the statutory right to sue for misrepresentation and/or to rescind (i.e., cancel) the franchise agreement for up to 60 days if there was an immaterial deficiency with the document, or up to two years after the agreement is entered into if there was a material deficiency or if no disclosure document was ever provided. The rescission remedy often results in major financial exposure to the franchisor, as the franchisor must compensate the franchisee for, among other items, all damages the franchisee has suffered in acquiring, establishing and operating the franchise. Note also that the rescission remedy may be exercised against any directors or officers of the franchisor who signed the disclosure document. The Canadian statutory right of rescission creates a punitive and costly remedy in favour of the franchisee, considered by many franchise lawyers to be the most serious consequence of non-compliance under any franchise legislation in the world.

The second principle is the duty of fair dealing, a duty that imposes on both the franchisor and the franchisee the obligation to act in good faith and in accordance with reasonable commercial standards in enforcing or performing the franchise agreement. If an alleged breach is in respect of an issue common to all or substantially all franchises within a specific system, the aggregate potential damages claim against a franchisor can run into the hundreds of millions of dollars, especially if the franchises combine their claims into a class action.

In our experience, the best course of action for a start-up, relatively new or seasoned franchisor to avoid rescission claims or claims for breach of the duty of fair dealing is to exercise extreme diligence in the preparation of disclosure documents and in the operation of the franchise system, utilizing experienced legal counsel for proactive and regular ongoing advice.

Is Your Business Ready for Franchising?

Over the years we have worked with many franchisors who developed franchise systems and started franchising for the right reasons and in the right manner. However, we have unfortunately also seen a number of franchisors start franchising for the wrong reasons and without proper preparation and advice. We have seen franchisors who have grown their systems utilizing the best practices in the industry, but unfortunately, we have also seen franchisors who have grown their systems without proper planning or direction.

While there are many questions and issues that could and should be asked and discussed with a business considering the launch of a franchise program, the core issues are relatively common. First, do you have a proven business system established through operating corporate stores? Second, does the business system lend itself to franchising in that it can be operated by an independent franchisee with reproducible and positive financial results? Third, is your intellectual property, particularly your trade-marks and domain names, protected or capable of being protected by law? Fourth, has an operations manual been prepared outlining the standards and procedures of operating the franchise? Finally, do you have the necessary resources, including personnel and financial capability, to retain appropriate professional advisors, prepare the relevant agreements and disclosure documents, train prospective franchises, grow the operations and promote the franchise system?

One thing is absolutely clear from our experience. Franchising should not be undertaken as a means of raising capital or testing a business system. There are too many uncertainties, costs and personal commitments required to launch a successful franchise system before risking your financial and operational resources and those of your franchises, not to mention risking the possibility of debilitating lawsuits.

Are You Partnering With the Right Franchise Law Firm for Success?

Creating, launching and operating a franchise system is a costly, complex and time-consuming venture. As a specialty practice area, franchising is relatively new to the legal profession as most franchise legislation in Canada has been in force for less than 10 years. However, some law firms have been active in franchising for many more years (for Osler, over 35 years) advising franchisors in respect of their documents and practices before franchise legislation existed.

There are a number of questions which a prospective franchisor should ask before retaining a law firm.

First, does the law firm have knowledge and experience in structuring a franchise system? There are many ways in which a franchise system can be rolled out, including single unit agreements, multi-unit agreements, development agreements, area representative agreements and joint ventures, it is essential that your legal advisors understand these different concepts and are able to apply them appropriately to your franchise system and the desired means of expanding your system.

Is your franchise law firm up-to-date with case law, current trends and best practices? Proactive and practical business advice must be coupled with legal considerations in order to develop the best possible franchise system with the least amount of risk.

Is your law firm ready, willing and able to deal with possible disputes as they arise? Franchisors should be well advised on how to avoid claims from franchises and, if a potential claim arises, how to deal with such claims with a view to resolving them before litigation commences. However, if litigation does arise, your law firm must have experienced litigators who have been involved in franchise disputes in order to provide you with the best tactical and legal advice.

Successful start-up franchisors understand that partnering with the right law firm is a key element of the initial investment required to launch their franchise system. Many prospective franchisors, however, do not comprehend the degree of legal expertise necessary to guide a franchisor through the relevant steps of developing, launching and establishing a franchise system. Franchise expertise is simply not enough. Being able to prepare a franchise agreement and disclosure document is only one step in a very complicated series of steps which are necessary from a legal perspective, and for franchise systems operated throughout Canada, national legal capability is fundamental. In our view, the best legal resources will be sourced in a national full service Canadian business law firm with expertise in all the relevant areas being applied to the franchise concept.

Experienced franchise law firms should also be able to advise their franchise clients on construction and leasing matters; security agreements, guarantees, letters of credit, promissory notes, and pre-authorized debit agreements; tax; marketing and promotions; general corporate matters; French language and other Quebec-specific issues; consumer protection legislation; gift cards; contests; packaging and labeling; customs and trade; privacy and anti-spam legislation; intellectual property; information systems; and social media.

What's In Your Franchise Agreement?

There is no such thing as a cookie cutter or standard form of franchise agreement. Franchise agreements must be prepared to reflect your franchise system and the manner in which you choose to operate your franchise program. No two franchise systems are the same. Our experience in assisting more than 400 franchise systems across a broad spectrum of product and service categories has given us a unique understanding of the variable business elements applicable in franchising in most business segments. For example, whether and how to include non-competition covenants in a hotel or real estate brokerage franchise agreement will differ considerably from non-competition covenants in a fast food restaurant franchise agreement.

Further, franchise agreements are not static documents, and what is current practice today differs considerably from what was current practice just a few years ago. Experienced franchise lawyers are fully up-to-date on case law developments, current trends, best practices and the application of other laws to franchising.

Your franchise lawyers must work with you in planning for the future, staying ahead of your competition, and proactively considering risk versus reward in including certain types of provisions in your franchise agreement.

Does Your Franchise Disclosure Document Measure Up?

When franchise disclosure legislation became more common in Canada, particularly after the enactment of Ontario's legislation in 2001, many lawyers prepared franchise disclosure documents on a one-for-all basis, without considering the fact that franchise disclosure must be tailored to the individual franchise being offered. As unique situations developed with respect to specific franchises being offered, we recognized early on that franchise disclosure documents must be customized for initial sales, resales or transfers, renewals and sales of corporate units. Only by carefully considering the comments made by our courts in reported cases has it become apparent that they are looking for customized disclosure documents with complete disclosure of all material facts specific to the actual franchise being offered. Your franchise disclosure document is not a static document, and the right law firm can help ensure your document reflects developing best practices and judicial interpretation of your statutory disclosure obligations. No franchisor should voluntarily expose itself to the significant risk of rescission and statutory damages when the costs of obtaining experienced legal counsel are relatively insignificant compared to the potential costs of a long, protracted and disruptive legal claim or worse still, class action. Experienced and proactive legal counsel can help you turn what may otherwise be considered an expensive and cumbersome document into a valuable and positive sales tool.

Our Concluding Comments

We hope this article will have been of assistance to you in understanding, very briefly, the various legal aspects involved in franchising and will have given you insight into how partnering with the right law firm experienced in franchising will help you to develop, operate and expand your franchise system with a comprehensive understanding of how to use and adopt the best practices in franchising.

We hope to be reading about your franchise system in the next book on successful Canadian franchise stories.

Osler, Hoskin & Harcourt LLP
Franchise Law Group
100 King Street West
1 First Canadian Place
Suite 6100, P.O. Box 50
Toronto, ON M5X 1B8

Phone: 416-362-2111
Fax: 416-862-6666
Email: counsel@osler.com
Website: www.osler.com

Sacke & Associates Inc.

5 PR Myths – Explained and Demystified

By John Sacke
Founder - Sacke & Associates Inc.

I've been in the public and media relations business my entire career – almost 25 years now – and while much has changed, the industry's tenets remain the same. Yes, we're in the age where social media seems to be the panacea to many and the sure-fire answer to any business malaise – "seems" and "panacea" being the operative words. Au contraire! Solid, honest and sustained communications is still the way to go. Every time.

While marketers are becoming savvier by the day, information is more accessible than ever before, the value of content has diminished, and location is almost irrelevant as geographical borders have all but disappeared. It's a difficult conundrum to say the least.

Based on almost a quarter century in the PR trenches in Europe, Asia and North

America, marketers generally understand and appreciate what public and media relations bring to the table. Except when they don't. And when they don't – they really don't. As PR practitioners, it's our collective jobs to deliver top top-notch service for reasonable fees, as well as to educate our clients.

Not long ago, the president of an Internet start-up who'd enjoyed a successful career told me he's always thought of PR as "the cheapest form of advertising." I think it may have been a compliment about the services we provide, but I hope he didn't mean it too literally. He was wrong on both counts – PR is not advertising and good PR is not cheap.

Misconceptions about public relations linger even among seasoned and sophisticated marketers. ***Here are five PR myths that persist, and my perspective on each.***

1. PR is Like Advertising, Only Cheaper

The two are as different from one another as chalk is from cheese. They're so distinct that they shouldn't even be compared, or, worse, pitted against one another. As I once heard, debating their merits is like arguing which is more important in a game of chess – offense or defense. It's a futile argument because each has a completely different function, and they work best in conjunction with each other.

And cheap? Not necessarily. It's the age-old adage – "You get what you pay for". Although a modest PR investment is inexpensive compared to, say, TV advertising, good PR is not actually cheap at all. Budgets vary widely, and many programs require significant out-of-pocket expenditures in addition to fees. Over the years, I've found that PR is as much (if not more) about strategy than it is about execution. It's happened time and time again; I'm approached to write a news release or two, and according to the client, that's all they need. More accurately, that's all they think they need. Peel back the onion a few layers, and it's clear they don't have a clue what to say, when to say it or even to whom they should be talking. And that is exactly why PR is not only not like advertising, but it's also not cheap. The key, of course, like anything else, is to match the need with the right PR resources and approach.

2. PR is Only About Getting the Word Out

This is only partially true; many marketers don't realize PR is a two-way street. While a successful public relations program is often designed to share important news, extol a brand, communicate a trend or a tell a business story, it should also function as an important mechanism of feedback and intelligence on what customers and influencers are thinking and saying. To note: Social media is now playing a key role in the feedback process. The savvy PR practitioner will then communicate this to the appropriate stakeholders who can then make better-informed decisions based on fact, rather than pure gut feeling.

Also, experience clearly tells me that implementing a PR program forces the company/client to think strategically and address some difficult-to-answer questions that they otherwise may have avoided addressing.

3. PR is Publicity. Preferably The Oprah Winfrey Show, or People Magazine

Sure, coverage in the media is often the happy result of an effective PR program, but a comprehensive, well-crafted plan covers so much more. It's not just a case of your PR guy calling some of his buddies in the media and the next thing you're on the front cover of *People Magazine*. That's just not how it works.

At the end of the day, it's about the story. Always was and always will be – and an astute PR person will let the client know that to get to the earned media outcomes, a solid, credible foundation must be laid. Overall brand positioning, building accurate media lists, sampling, media strategy, relationship-building, key messaging, etc. – all are critical for successful results.

When the publicity finally breaks, it's not usually a magic bullet. In as much as one swallow rarely makes a summer, one media hit (no matter how big), rarely changes the world. Rather, it's all about sustainability, frequency, and credibility, and that often takes months, if not years to build. Yes, PR people trade control for credibility (another reason why PR is not like advertising). And what PR experts don't like to admit is that Oprah's producers rarely take ideas from PR people anyway. Rather, they look for news based on trends or something they see or hear.

4. The Internet has Made PR Cheaper and Easier

Nonsense. Companies have been conned into believing that they can electronically send press releases for "almost free", or in some cases, even worse, "completely free". The idea of "free distribution" or "free anything" is false. Somebody (presumably paid) has to write the press releases. Then you pay someone to make follow-up calls when nobody in the media notices the releases. Your free press releases end up costing more than back in the old days when people had to stuff paper in envelopes.

True, you can email information to personal contacts or post it on various industry-based websites (high traffic websites charge these days). All it takes is time – but time is money! Also consider whether your email and posting efforts are worth the trouble of attracting just a few potential readers.

So, you might end up paying a wire service to distribute the release far and wide at say $400 a time. Go ask the wire services, whom I have nothing against. They'll proudly tell you they're sending out more news releases than ever before. *(Read: your release is competing for attention with tens of thousands of others)*. There's nothing wrong with press releases – in fact most of them are so benign they have minimal impact, except to drain your budget. While the news stream is important, the release itself is a commodity.

Press releases don't add up to a strategic PR program, and the impact of any one release is likely to be low. If you're paying someone to put together a news release or two from time to time and doing nothing else, you're wasting your money. Fact is the average press release costs $1,800 to prepare and distribute, and a large percentage of them are simply deleted before the media ever reads the first sentence. The media are busy people after all, contrary to popular belief. Rather than a stand-alone, a news release should be an important consideration (and part) of an integrated marketing communications plan.

5. PR Drives Sales

I cringe when I hear a client or marketer say they've put their ad budget into PR because it's a cheaper way to generate sales. I can't stress it enough – PR (while it may generate sales leads) is not designed for demand generation. Period. Despite some spectacular exceptions, public relations programs add to brand visibility, enhance reputation and deliver credibility over time. When it comes to driving sales, without a built-in sampling program, an on-the-ball sales force, attractive pricing, superb customer service, a kick-ass product and other promotional pieces, PR initiatives alone will nearly always fall short, particularly because frequency is nearly impossible to achieve with publicity alone.

The Bottom Line

A good public relations plan includes a broad range of efforts and activities which must work in conjunction with advertising and marketing/sales support programs. All of these tools have to work together, in the same direction and with the proper mixture and timing, to achieve an overall corporate and marketing goal. If they don't, time, money, and effort is wasted.

Sacke & Associates Inc.
7030 Woodbine Avenue, Suite 500
Markham, Ontario, Canada L3R 6G2

Phone: 416-493-5723
Fax: 866-557-5196
Email: enquiries@sackepr.com
Website: http://www.sackepr.com

Recommended Resources

Felicia Pizzonia

Author

Felicia Pizzonia has spent many years cultivating her national and international publishing and marketing expertise. As an entrepreneur, Felicia has assisted several hundred authors publish and market their books on an international level. Her unique ability to demystify the book industry and walk authors through the publishing process has endeared her to many authors and led to long-term, mutually beneficial relationships; thereby enhancing their businesses. Her dreams of entrepreneurship and inspiring others to accomplish their goals fuelled her desire to write her first book, titled: ***Babes in Business Suits: Success Secrets of the Top Women Entrepreneurs of the World***. She is a partner in the Ultimate Publishing House (TUPH) and mainly publishes non-fiction books, helping professionals "brand" themselves and their business. Felicia is also the president of The Ultimate Branding Agency, a company that helps entrepreneurial type authors and businesses market and promote themselves via published books, e-books and social media campaigns. Felicia has worked closely with Bob Proctor, a well-known philosopher and motivational speaker, as well as some of the world's top entrepreneurs including Anthony Robbins, Donald Trump, and Henk Diebrink.

Felicia's first book, ***Babes in Business Suits: Success Secrets of the Top Women Entrepreneurs of the World*** (2009) is a testament to her desire to help business people succeed. Since the book appealed mostly to female entrepreneurs, Felicia planned to write a success book showcasing both men and women in her future endeavours. Her next book initially showcased *Canadian Babes in the Franchise World*, but after taking into consideration her plan to incorporate the success of both men and women in business, Felicia immediately created a new title, hence the birth of ***Great Canadian Franchise Stories***' first edition. During the making of the book, Felicia generated a list of some of Canada's top franchisors whom she wanted to invite to be featured in the book; one of whom was Dawn Mucci of Lice Squad Canada. Dawn quickly realized how incredible the concept of the book was and asked Felicia if she could collaborate with her on the project, Felicia accepted the proposal and the two joined forces.

Felicia also hosts seminars on *Personal Branding Success*; *How to Write a Book in 90 Days* workshops, and the Ultimate Achievement Course™ for teens and adults. Felicia sits on the board of a federal not for profit organization called *Get fit, Eat right, Live life Together* (GELtogether.org); an organization educating kids and teens on healthy initiatives.

Dawn Mucci

Dawn Mucci was born in the Yorkville area of Toronto and grew up in the West End neighbourhood of High Park. From a young age Dawn was very drawn to helping others and to being creative. As an only child, she had a lot of time to use her imagination. A natural born leader, Dawn recognized early in life the power of persuasion, negotiation and cooperation. She began her entrepreneurial career at the age of six selling lemonade and toys at the foot of her flat above the record store in Toronto where she lived with her father. Seeing her ability to earn a dollar on her own was a thrill and became a regular means of which she often used to raise money to buy the things her single father was unable to afford to buy her. Dawn was also drawn to writing and singing and it came naturally to her. Music and writing were an outlet that she used to cope and to celebrate. She has written many songs, poems and short stories and continues to do so. In high school Dawn excelled at English, entrepreneurship, performing arts and sports. After high school, Dawn ventured into the work force but always felt unfulfilled and had a deep calling in her soul to create something of value and something of her very own. Her first business, New Dawn Aromatherapy, lead her into working with and helping people in a health capacity, creating blends of essential oils for bath, body and environmental care. When this business did not work she took a job with the city. After an accident and a separation she found herself on assistance as a single mother with a young child to support, struggling to get by. It was at this time that head lice affected her and her natural entrepreneurial spirit quickly recognized the opportunity to use this situation, her creativity and desire help others and to start a business. Little did she know or realize that what she started would become a franchise and in turn would add value and fulfillment to other people's lives. Dawn Mucci founded Lice Squad Canada in 2001 and continues to use her talent, creativity, and leadership to help people through this business and in her other business and professional endeavours.

RECYCLED
Paper made from recycled material
FSC® C103567
FSC www.fsc.org

Printed on Enviro 100% post-consumer EcoLogo certified paper, processed chlorine free and manufactured using biogas energy.

100%
PERMANENT
BIO GAS ENERGY